# COLLECTIONS

### A Harcourt Reading Program

## Bright Voices

Orlando  Boston  Dallas  Chicago  San Diego

Visit *The Learning Site!*

**www.harcourtschool.com**

**Photo Credits**

(t) = top, (b) = bottom, (c) = center, (l) = left, (r) = right, (bkgd) = background.
Page 30, S.S. Gallery/National Baseball Hall of Fame Library; 31(l) AP/Wide World Photos; 31(r), Milo Stewart, Jr./National Baseball Hall of Fame Library; 32(l & r), AP/Wide World Photos; 32(c), Milo Stewart, Jr./National Baseball Hall of Fame Library; 32-33(bat), Ken Kinzie / Harcourt; 34-35 Ken Kinzie / Harcourt; 33, New York Daily News; 34(r), Corbis/Bettmann-UPI; 34-35 Ken Kinzie / Harcourt; 34(l), Michael Groen Phography; 35(r), Corbis/Bettmann; 36, AP/Wide World Photos; 37(frame,cap), Ken Kinzie / Harcourt; 70, 73, 74, 76, Doug Dukane/Harcourt; 78(l), Gerry Ellis/ENP Images; 78(r), Daniel J. Cox/Natural Exposures; 79 & 80(t), Gerry Ellis/ENP Images; 80(b), Daniel J. Cox/Natural Exposures; 81(t), John Chellman/Animals, Animals; 81(b) & 82, Gerry Ellis/ENP Images; 83(t), Daniel J. Cox/Natural Exposures; 83(b), Rob Brindamour/National Geographic Images; 84, 85 & (bkgrd), Daniel J. Cox/Natural Exposures; 110-111, The Stock Market; 111(inset), Thomas H. Brakefield/The Stock Market; 111(tr), Tim Davis/The Stock Market; 112-113(both), 114, Tom Brakefield/The Stock Market; 115, First Light/Zephyr Images; 116, Robert Winslow/Animals, Animals; 117, Daniel J. Cox/Tony Stone Images; 198-204 (all), Lawrence Migdale.

# CONTENTS

# Gram's Plant Parade

by Susan McCloskey
illustrated by Melanie Hall

My name is Blake, and this is my gram. Gram adores plants.

Gram plants in any vacant vase. She plants in hats and caps. She plants in cake pans and brass vats. She plants in frames and crates.

Look! One plant is sprouting in a skate with no mate!

"Blake!" says my gram. "Look at the
station on the corner. Do you see what I see?"
"No, Gram. What do you see?" I ask.
"Vacant land to plant!" says Gram.

Gram takes a sack. I take the spade. We go to the station on the corner.

Gram has bulbs in the sack. She takes bulbs from her pockets, too.

"Now hand me my spade, Blake," she says, "and stand back. I have to plant!"

As Gram plants, we attract stares. Recognizing that I am anxious, Gram pats me on the back.

"Blake, aren't you glad we're sprucing up the station?" she says. "I can't stand a drab, bare landscape!"

"Gram, you amaze me! When will the bulbs be sprouting?" I ask.

"In the future," Gram says. "Then we'll see a plant parade!"

At last the future comes to pass!

Gram and I go to gaze at her plant parade. Now it's the plants that attract stares! One man thanks Gram for sprucing up the corner.

"Will you retire from planting now, Gram?" I ask.
"Retire? Not me!" Gram gazes around the square.
"Look!" she says. "I see vacant land!"
Now I want to share Gram's plant craze.
I know a new plant parade is in our future!

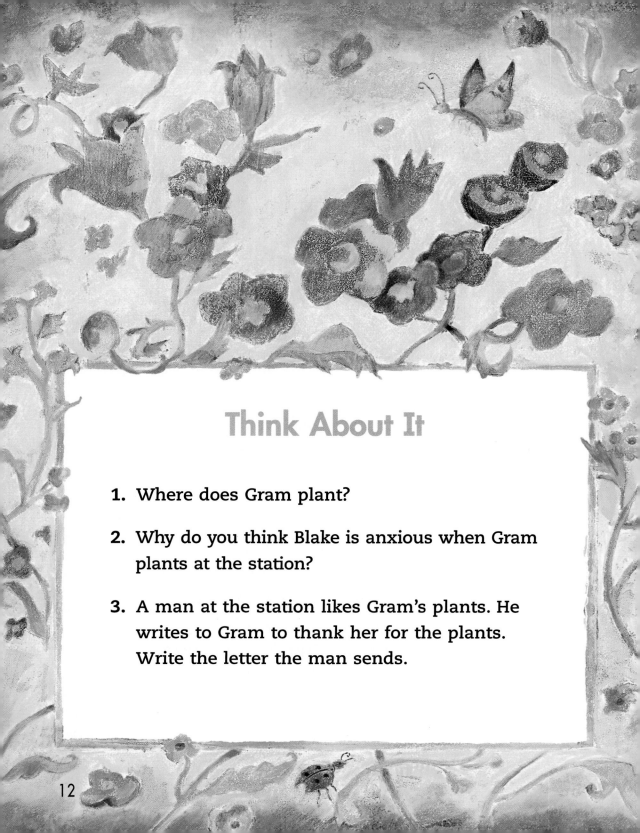

## Think About It

1. Where does Gram plant?

2. Why do you think Blake is anxious when Gram plants at the station?

3. A man at the station likes Gram's plants. He writes to Gram to thank her for the plants. Write the letter the man sends.

# Narrative Elements

A story has three important parts, or narrative elements. The **setting** is when and where the story takes place. The **characters** are the people in the story. The **plot** is what happens in the story.

The story map below shows the narrative elements of "Gram's Plant Parade."

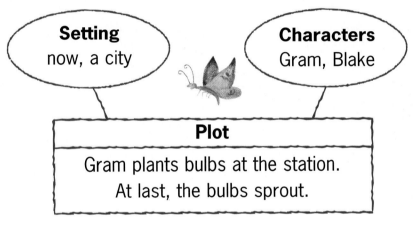

**Setting**
now, a city

**Characters**
Gram, Blake

**Plot**

Gram plants bulbs at the station.
At last, the bulbs sprout.

Which narrative element would change if Blake's friends helped Gram plant? Which narrative element would change if some dogs dug up the bulbs before they could sprout?

Plan a story of your own. Make a story map to show the narrative elements of your story.

# CLICK!

by Celeste Albright   illustrated by Michele Noiset

All the kids in our class like Miss Wise. She makes us smile!

"Look at this pin that Kim gave me!" Miss Wise says. "Isn't it a kick?" She has the pin on her hat. It's a fish pin, and the fish has big pink lips.

Mike Briggs says, "Smile, Miss Wise!"

Miss Wise grins.

That's Mike for you. Click, click, click, all the time.

"I collect pins," Miss Wise says. "Collecting them is what I do in my leisure time. It can have its disappointments, when I can't get the pin I want. The solution is perseverance!

"See if you like being collectors, kids. Bring a collection to class when you can."

Mike visits Tim to see what he's collecting.

"I have nine hats," Tim says. He has on six of them. "Is this a collection?"

"It looks like a collection to me," Mike says.

"Mike, what will you do for a collection?" Tim asks.

"It's not a problem," says Mike. "You'll see. Smile!"

Mike rides off on his bike to see Jill.

"I'm a stamp collector," says Jill. "I like sitting and looking at my stamps."

"That white one with the plane is my favorite," Mike says.

Jill picks it up.

"Smile, Jill!" says Mike.

CLICK!

Then Mike bikes over to Linda's.
"I collect pigs!" says Linda.
"Pigs?" Mike looks uneasy.
"Don't they stink a bit? Do your
neighbors get mad? You could
compromise with them and collect
cats. Cats would be no problem."
Linda chortles. "My pigs are no
problem to our neighbors." She
invites Mike in to see them.

Linda has pigs of all sizes. Many were gifts. She has ticking pigs, big pigs, and five pink pigs.

Linda picks up her favorite, a pig in a hat and wig.

"What do you collect, Mike?" she asks.

Mike grins. He says, "You'll see in class. Smile, Miss Pig in a Wig!"

CLICK!

19

"What's in there, Mike?" the kids ask.

"You are!" Mike says. "Take a look!" There's Tim in his hats. There are Jill and Linda. All the kids are there.

"That's quite a collection!" Miss Wise says. "A smile collection! I like it. Now, you smile, Mike!"

And what a fine smile it is.

CLICK!

## Think About It

**1.** What does Mike collect? How does he collect them?

**2.** Why do you think Miss Wise asks her class to be collectors?

**3.** Write a news story about the collections made by the kids in Miss Wise's class.

# A Troublesome NOSE

by Linda Lott    illustrated by Russ Wilson

Miss Jones's class is planning a holiday pageant. Ron is glad that they are going to act out his favorite book.

In the book, a fox, a dog, and a frog make a visit to a tropical land. They plan a fine holiday, but troublesome problems come up.

Ron hopes to get a role, and he is not disappointed. He gets to be the fox. He has the greatest lines—they're all jokes. All the kids like the fox.

Ron says his lines over and over so he will not make a mistake on stage. His mom and dad will be coming to the pageant.

The time comes for the dress rehearsal, and Miss Jones gives out the costumes. Ron's is a fake fox nose.

The long nose looks fine, but it's a troublesome nose. The problem is that it flip-flops up and down. It flips up, and Ron can't see. It flops down, and it's over his lips. When Ron says his lines, all that comes out is "Mmm, mmm, mmm." The kids can't get the jokes.

Ron jogs home, swinging the nose on its string. When he gets inside, Mom looks up.

"What a fine nose!" she says.

"It's not fine at all," Ron says. He pops the nose on and says his lines. The nose flip-flops up and down. Mom can't get anything but "Mmm, mmm, mmm."

Dad grins and hands Ron some tape. "You'll have to fix it so it doesn't flip-flop," he says.

"I hope I can fix it in time," Ron says.

At the pageant, it's time for the fox to be seen. Ron lopes onto the stage. All the kids smile.

Mom and Dad gaze attentively at the nose. What if it still slips? Can Ron cope with it?

The nose does slip! First it rides up so Ron can't see. Ron gropes for it, and the kids all grin. Then the nose slips down over Ron's lips.

"Mmm, mmm, mmm," says the fox.

The kids are having a fit. Ron grins back at them. Then he puts the nose up on top. Now he can say his lines just fine. He does not make one mistake.

Mom and Dad clap and clap. Then they make a visit to the stage.

"Good job, Ron!" they say. "You came up with a fine solution to your problem."

"I like that fox role," says Ron. "The jokes are all good ones. The troublesome nose was the greatest joke of all!"

# Think About It

1. What is Ron's role in the holiday pageant? Why does he like that role?

2. Why is the big nose the greatest joke of all?

3. After the play, Ron writes a postcard to his friend. He tells all about the troublesome nose. Write the postcard Ron sends.

# Prefixes and Suffixes

Knowing about prefixes and suffixes can help you read new words. A **prefix** is a word part added to the beginning of a word. A **suffix** is a word part added to the end of a word. They can change the meaning or part of speech of a word.

| Prefixes |
| --- |
| un-  re-  im- |

| Suffixes |
| --- |
| -some  -ly  -ful |

Read these sentences. What prefix can you find in the first sentence? What suffix can you find in the second sentence?

**Ron was unhappy with the fake nose.**
**It was a troublesome prop.**

Now read these sentences. In each sentence, find the word with a prefix or a suffix. What do these words mean?

**The kids had to remake some of the props.**
**They worked quickly.**
**Miss Jones was helpful.**

Put together the prefix or suffix and the base word. Write your own sentence with each new word you make.

| un-  kind |
| --- |
| re-  do |

| hope  -ful |
| --- |
| polite  -ly |

# Joe DiMaggio

## One of Baseball's Greatest

by Tomás Castillo

Joe DiMaggio, the son of immigrant parents, began his baseball career in 1936. He came to the New York Yankees when Lou Gehrig was with them. DiMaggio was 21 and glad to make such a fine team.

The Yankees' manager had hopes for DiMaggio, but Yankees fans were upset. The new man had a bad leg. People asked, "Can he run around the bases? Can he hit in Yankee Stadium?"

In no time, people got to like DiMaggio. They came to the stadium to see him. He was modest, but his hitting was making him a favorite of Yankees fans. Baseball fans from all over agreed that Joe DiMaggio was a tremendous find.

DiMaggio got 206 hits in 1936, and 29 of them were home runs! The Yankees' manager noted that DiMaggio was valuable to the team, and his salary went up.

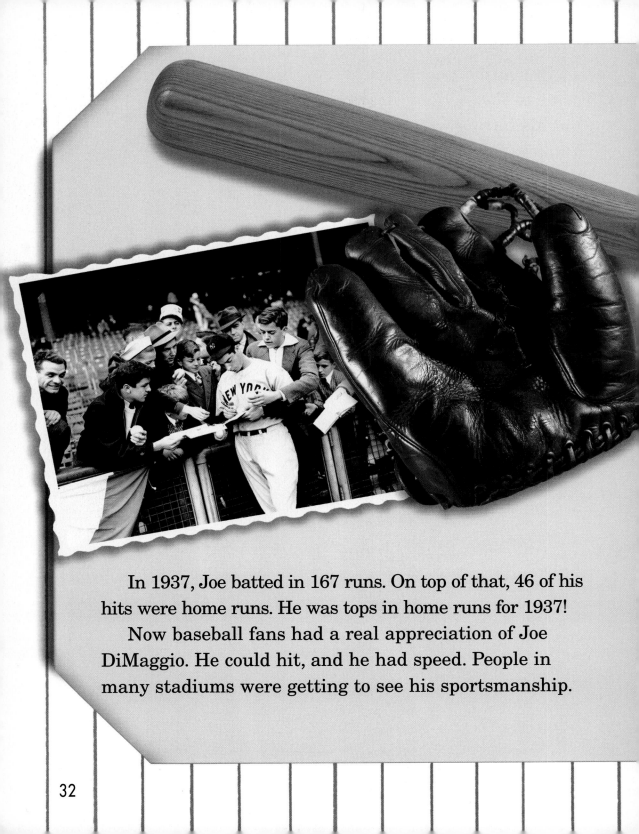

In 1937, Joe batted in 167 runs. On top of that, 46 of his hits were home runs. He was tops in home runs for 1937!

Now baseball fans had a real appreciation of Joe DiMaggio. He could hit, and he had speed. People in many stadiums were getting to see his sportsmanship.

DiMaggio still had a "hot bat" in 1938 and 1939. His home runs went down, but his batting went up. In 1939, it was the best in all of baseball.

In 1940, his batting fell off a little. The Yankees slid out of their top spot. The upset manager of the Yankees had to hope his team could be tops again in 1941.

**FINAL** ★★★★ **DAILY**  **NEWS** The LARGEST CIRCULATION IN AMERICA

NEW YORK'S — PICTURE NEWSPAPER — Entered as 2nd class matter, Post Office, New York, N.Y.

Copyright 1936 by News Syndicate Co. Inc. Reg. U. S. Pat. Off.

Vol. 17. No. 268    48 Pages      New York, Monday, May 4, 1936      2 Cents

# DIMAGGIO SMACKS 3 HITS
# IN DEBUT; YANKS WIN, 14-5

Story on Page 42

The Yankees did win back the top spot, but
Joe DiMaggio outdid his team. On May 15, 1941,
in a game with the Chicago White Sox, he began an
amazing hitting streak. First he got at least one hit in
each of ten games in a row. Then it was 20 games.
When was Joe DiMaggio going to stop getting hits?

For 56 games, DiMaggio got hits. He did not miss one game. On July 17, 1941, in a game with the Cleveland Indians, his hitting streak ended.

Baseball fans will not forget the courageous sportsmanship of Joe DiMaggio. He had a lot of heat on him in 1941, but he met the test. His feat of getting a hit in 56 games still stands.

JOSEPH PAUL DI MAGGIO
NEW YORK A.L.1936 TO 1951

HIT SAFELY IN 56 CONSECUTIVE GAMES
FOR MAJOR LEAGUE RECORD 1941. HIT 2
HOME-RUNS IN ONE INNING 1936. HIT 3
HOME-RUNS IN ONE GAME (3 TIMES). HOLDS
NUMEROUS BATTING RECORDS. PLAYED IN
10 WORLD SERIES (51 GAMES) AND 11 ALL
STAR GAMES. MOST VALUABLE PLAYER
A.L. 1939, 1941, 1947.

Joe DiMaggio retired from baseball in 1951. The Yankees were sad to see him go. So were baseball fans from New York and all over. In 1955, he was voted into the Baseball Hall of Fame.

DiMaggio had a fine life. He was 84 when it ended on March 8, 1999. He had given a lot to the game he cared about. Baseball fans will not forget Joe DiMaggio. He was one of the greatest.

# Think About It

1. Why was Joe DiMaggio voted into the Baseball Hall of Fame?

2. Why did the fans like Joe DiMaggio?

3. Suppose you were in the stands when Joe DiMaggio got a hit in his amazing hitting streak. At home, you wanted to tell about the game in your diary. Write your diary entry.

# BLIZZARD SEASON

by Kaye Gager    illustrated by Karen Pritchett

When I woke up, I could tell right away there was a problem. No sunshine came in, and blasts of wind were shaking the cabin.

I got up and looked outdoors. A blizzard, of all things! How could this be? It was the middle of May! When we went to bed, it was springtime.

I got the children up and helped them dress. Ma bustled around, making us a pot of hot tea with honey. We all sat near the stove with our mugs.

"Children," Ma said, "this is a big storm. We'll have to do our chores when it lets up a bit. Pa will be back this afternoon, but that could be too late!"

"How can we be having a blizzard, Ma?" I asked. "It's May and all my plants are up!"

Ma said, "Sometimes we do have a spring storm. You children just haven't seen one. Your plants may be all right, Bess."

When the snow stopped for a while, we did our chores frantically. Jen and Jeff dug a path to the hens. Little Tim held the sack of feed. Ma and I dragged some cut logs inside by the stove.

All the while, I was thinking of my hidden plants. I hoped the deep snow was not freezing their new little stems and leaves.

In no time, the blizzard was back. Stinging snow scoured our cheeks and noses.

Ma staggered over to me.

"Bess, get the children," she said. "It's time to stop. We did what we could."

We were thankful to be inside our snug home. Ma got out her flute, and we sang all our favorite tunes. In the afternoon Pa made it home safe from his trip.

By the time we went to bed, the blizzard was over. Just a gentle breeze ruffled the snow.

When we got up, it was very still outdoors. Pa and I did the chores while Ma made us a hot meal. We ate it by the stove as the children ran around restlessly.

"Can we go outdoors? It's not bad out there now," Jen said earnestly.

Ma looked out. "You can go, but you must keep your hats on!"

We put on our outdoor things fast, hats and all.
Little Tim looked so cute in his hat with kitten ears!

We had the greatest time outside! We waded in
the deep snow. We slipped and slid. We pulled Tim in
a box and made snow people. Jen and I hid, and
when Jeff came near, we pelted him with snow. That
gave him an excuse to get us! Whap!

Then Tim said, "Look! There's the sun!" We looked
up. Tim was right!

By afternoon, the sun was hot. Our snow people melted, but we were glad to have spring back. There was mud all over, but the breeze smelled fresh.

Ma came out. "Spring storms come and go fast," she said, "but this one was amazing."

Then she said, "Look down, Bess!" I did, and there in the mud were green sprouts, green stems, and green leaves! Ma was right. My plants didn't freeze after all.

I gave Ma a big hug. It was May, and it would be June next. I hoped earnestly that blizzard season was over!

# Think About It

1. What makes the storm so amazing?

2. Why hasn't Bess seen a spring storm before?

3. Make a web with words that tell what the main character, Bess, likes and what she does. Use the web to write a paragraph about Bess.

# Journey by Caravan

by Sharon Fear
illustrated by Kung Lu

Some men were getting ready for a journey by caravan. Their camels could hear them as they argued over their packing.

"I hate to travel with those men," said one camel. "They will be arguing all the time. They just can't agree on anything. One WILL do this, and one MUST do that! When we come to a big sand dune, some WILL walk to this side, some MUST walk to that side."

A tall camel nodded. "When we come to a steep hill, some WILL walk up the hill in this spot. Some MUST walk up in that spot!"

"At night," said a fat camel, "some of them will decide it's time to make camp. Some will decide to keep walking over unfamiliar land. They won't know where they're going and may fall into a thicket of bushes. They may think they're in a forest!"

"We must help them," said the smallest camel. "We must get them to act as one and put an end to this problem."

All the camels agreed.

The men and animals set off on their journey. This time, when they came to a dune, all the camels walked to one side. The men called and begged them, but the animals acted as one.

When they came to a steep hill, all the camels went up at one spot. The men pulled and tugged, but the animals acted as one.

At nightfall the animals halted by some small, bare trees. If this was a forest, the clearing was the biggest part! Some of the men, as always, wanted to keep going, but the forest would have to do. Not one man could get his camel to walk on.

That night, they all shared the chores. One man fed the animals, one made the campfire, one made the meal, and so on. For the first time, they worked as a team.

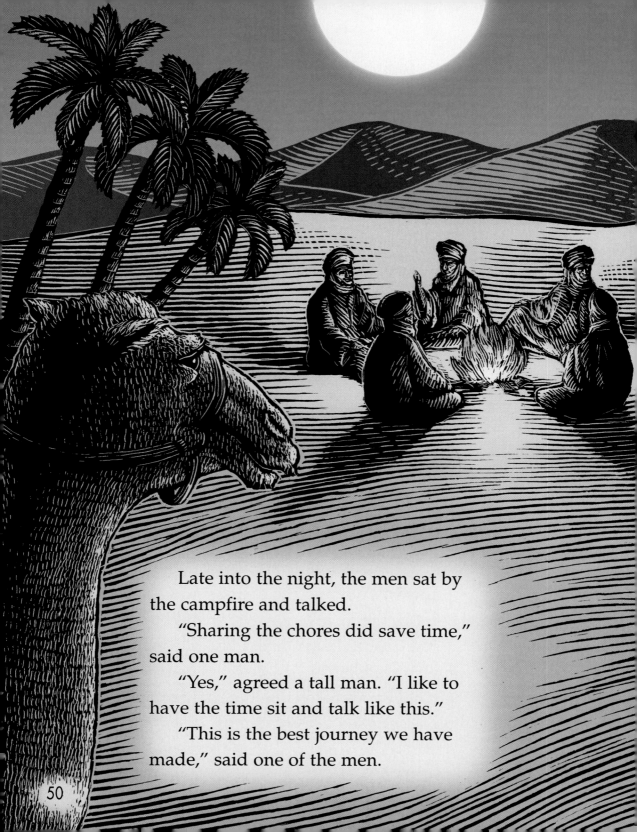

Late into the night, the men sat by the campfire and talked.

"Sharing the chores did save time," said one man.

"Yes," agreed a tall man. "I like to have the time sit and talk like this."

"This is the best journey we have made," said one of the men.

"Could it be," asked the first man, "that unity is best?"

"Yes! Yes!" said all the men. "Unity IS best!"

"How wise of us to see it!" said the tall man.

The men talked about future trips. They looked to their next journey with anticipation.

So did the camels.

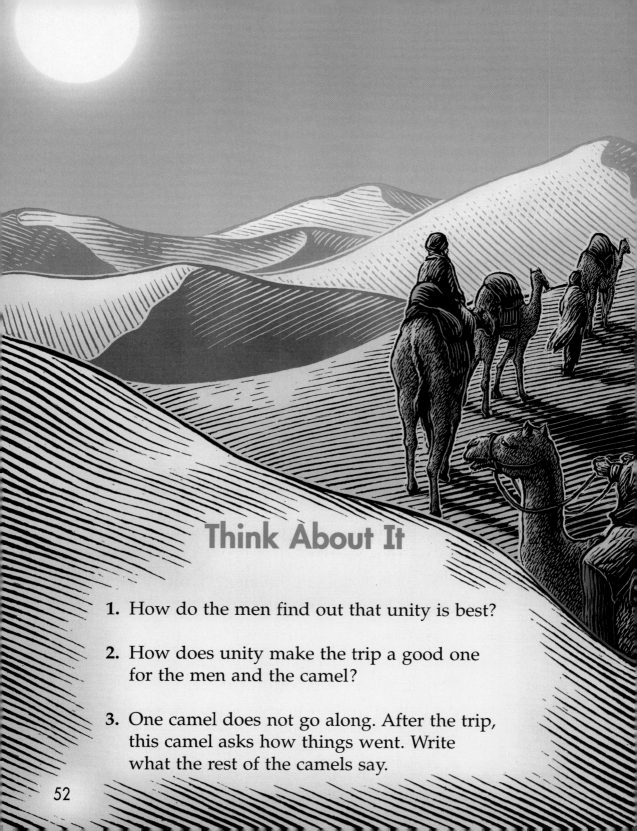

## Think About It

1. How do the men find out that unity is best?

2. How does unity make the trip a good one
   for the men and the camel?

3. One camel does not go along. After the trip,
   this camel asks how things went. Write
   what the rest of the camels say.

# Predict Outcomes

As you read this story, did you think about what would happen on the journey? If you did, you were **making predictions**.

To make a prediction, you think about what you read in the story. You think about what you already know.

Then you put these things together to predict what will happen.

Making predictions can help you be a more active reader. This web shows how you could make a prediction while you read "Journey by Caravan."

**What I Read**
The camels want to get the men to act as one.

**What I Know**
Camels are stubborn. Most times, they get their way.

**Prediction**
The camels will do something to make the men act as one.

Reread the last page of "Journey by Caravan." Think about what you read there and about what you know. Draw a web to show your predictions about the next trip that the men and their camels will take.

# Green Tomatoes

by Charlene Norman

illustrated by Liz Conrad

Martin skidded his bike to a stop, making a haze of dust. "Here's Mom's list," he said to Nick. "Can I feed the carp in your pond?"

Nick smiled as he filled a sack with tomatoes, carrots, and beans. "Now you can go feed the carp."

Martin ran to the backyard. "You have the greatest garden!" he called.

Carla and Lil got what they needed from Nick's stand. "We're making pickles," said Carla.

"I like pickles," Nick said, "if they're a little sweet."

"I like frogs," said Lil. "They're green."

"We have some in the pond. Go visit them if you like," Nick said.

Miss Marlene gave Nick some money for tomatoes. "May I sit on your garden seat for a while?" she asked. "I like to inhale the sweet smells there."

Nick smiled and agreed. This was the season for garden visits.

In the afternoon, Nick did some of his favorite things in his garden. He measured neat lines for the next part of his garden mural. He fed the carp in his backyard pond. He trimmed the lavender and the trumpet vines by the seat in the corner. He weeded the bed of beans.

Then he stopped. "Who stole the tomatoes off my plants?" he yelled. "They were still small and green—they were for my next big harvest!"

Did one of his neighbors pick them? Then Nick saw a line of lavender petals leaving the garden. He decided to track them.

The petals led Nick to Carla and Lil's yard. Carla was sitting on the steps, reading. Lil was swinging a plastic bat.

"Help!" he called. "My green tomatoes are missing from my tomato bed. Have you seen them?"

"I haven't seen them," said Carla, "but I'll help you look." They looked in Lil's wagon and sandbox, but there were no tomatoes.

Then Carla saw Lil hit a green ball. "Lil has lots of small plastic balls, but no green ones!" she said. Carla and Nick ran over. They grabbed small green tomatoes out of Lil's box.

"Mine!" yelled Lil. "I like the green ones best!"

Nick held up a tomato. "I can't sell this. It's too green. It's useless." He sniffed and blinked.

Carla looked down. She felt bad. "I didn't see Lil taking your tomatoes," she said. "I'll give you the money for them."

"No," said Nick. "I can't take money for green tomatoes."

After a week, Carla and Lil came to Nick's stand, grinning. They gave Nick a jar of pickled green tomatoes.

Nick bit into one. "This isn't useless. This is quite a treat!" He gave Carla a wide grin. "I know I can sell these!"

Then Nick patted Lil's back. "Next year, you can help me harvest more green tomatoes to pickle. But not all of them!"

# Think About It

1. Why do Carla and Lil give Nick a jar of pickled green tomatoes?

2. Why won't Nick and Lil harvest *all* the green tomatoes for pickles next year?

3. Next year Nick will make a poster to tell his neighbors that it is harvest time. Make a poster that Nick could use.

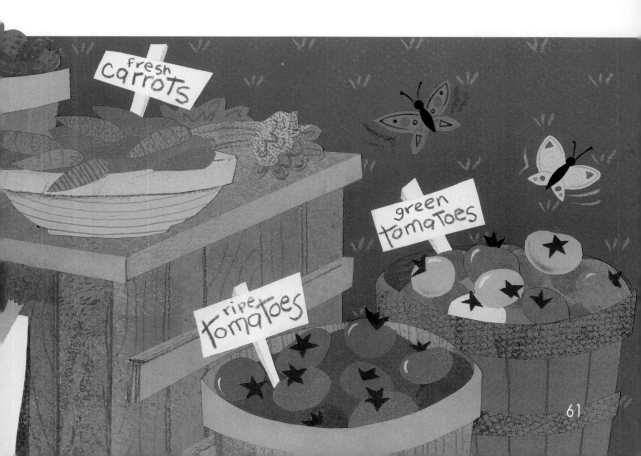

# Bringing Back the
# PUFFINS

by Caren B. Stelson
illustrated by Paul Mirocha

Spring has come back to Egg Rock, but will the puffins come back too? A man named Steve Kress watches and hopes. For a long time, no puffins had nested on these uninhabited rocks. Then Kress started a plan to bring them back. He hopes his puffin plan will go right.

Over 100 years ago, puffins nested on Egg Rock. Kress wanted to see them there again. In 1973, he and his team went to a land that has many puffins. They collected puffin chicks, being very careful with them, and then rushed them back to Egg Rock.

Steve Kress and his team acted as parents to tend the puffin chicks. They made a village of burrows for the chicks to nestle in. They fed them fresh fish and kept them safe from dangers, such as gulls. Kress and his team made good puffin parents!

One night the puffins came out of their village of burrows. It was time for them to venture into the sea. Each made a wobbling flight, splashed in, and went out into the dark night.

Would the puffins come back to breed and to tend their chicks? Kress hoped that in two to three years, they would instinctively do this.

There are many dangers for puffins at sea. They can be eaten if a gull spies them. They can be stranded in fishing nets. They can be harmed by big waves.

Yet puffins are made for sea life. They can dive deep and swim fast. They use their wings to swim and their webbed feet to steer. They catch fish with their sharp beaks. Kress hoped at least some of his puffins would make it back to Egg Rock.

Now Steve Kress sits on Egg Rock, keeping watch and hoping his plan was not just a dream. He watches for a long, long time.

Then Kress spies a black speck in flight. The speck gets bigger and bigger as it sweeps over the sea. Kress leaps to his feet and yells to his team. The puffins have come back to Egg Rock!

# Think About It

1. How did Steve Kress and his team help puffin chicks live on Egg Rock?

2. Why did the adult puffins come back to Egg Rock?

3. What else do you want to know about puffins? Write three questions you would like to ask Steve Kress.

# Cause and Effect

The puffins came back to Egg Rock because of the work of Steve Kress. Thinking about why things happen can help you understand what you read. Why something happens is a **cause**. What happens is the **effect**.

This chart shows a cause and an effect from "Bringing Back the Puffins."

| Cause | → | Effect |
|---|---|---|
| Kress and his team kept the baby puffins safe. | | The baby puffins got big and strong. |

Sometimes an effect has several causes. Sometimes a cause has several effects.

Look at this picture. To find an effect, ask yourself "What is happening?" To find a cause, ask "Why is it happening?" Write about your ideas.

# Smart as a Fox

by Celeste Albright
illustrated by Alexi Natchev

## CAST

**Narrator**
**Mr. Gray**, a farmer
**Mrs. Gray**

**Abigail**, a cat
**Duke**, a dog
**Sidney**, a fox

**SETTING:** the Grays' farm

**NARRATOR:** Hail, neighbors! You're just in time to see a terrific play. You'll like it, I promise! I'm the Narrator. That means I stay here, offstage, and explain, explain, explain. (*Shrugs.*) Well, at least I get to sit down now and then.

**DUKE:** Grrrrrrrr!

**NARRATOR:** Okay, okay! I get the message. Let's start the play!

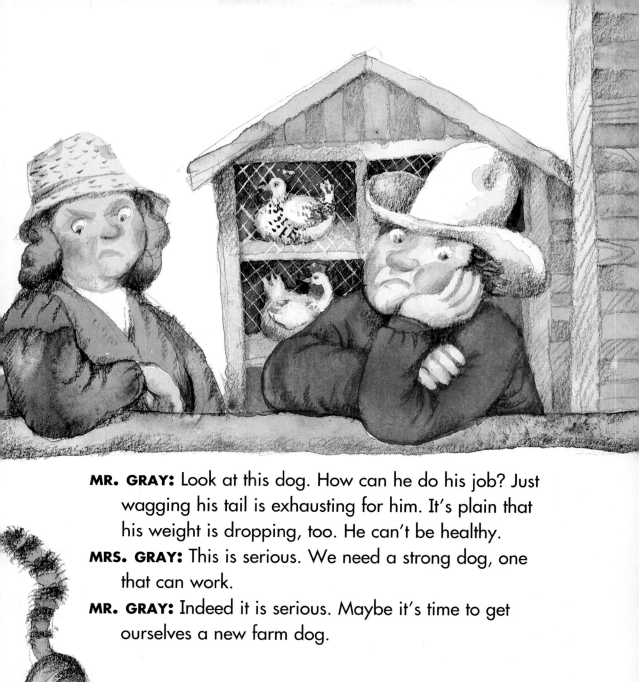

**MR. GRAY:** Look at this dog. How can he do his job? Just wagging his tail is exhausting for him. It's plain that his weight is dropping, too. He can't be healthy.

**MRS. GRAY:** This is serious. We need a strong dog, one that can work.

**MR. GRAY:** Indeed it is serious. Maybe it's time to get ourselves a new farm dog.

71

**MRS. GRAY:** You know, the cat looks unhealthy as well. She used to be as quick as an acrobat. Now look how frail and fragile she is! She's lost weight, too, and she hasn't nabbed a rat in days.

**ABIGAIL** (*to Duke*): It's a conspiracy. They want to get rid of us!

**DUKE** (*Whining*): Nnn-nnn-nnn!

**ABIGAIL:** Shh! Stop whining! It'll just encourage them.

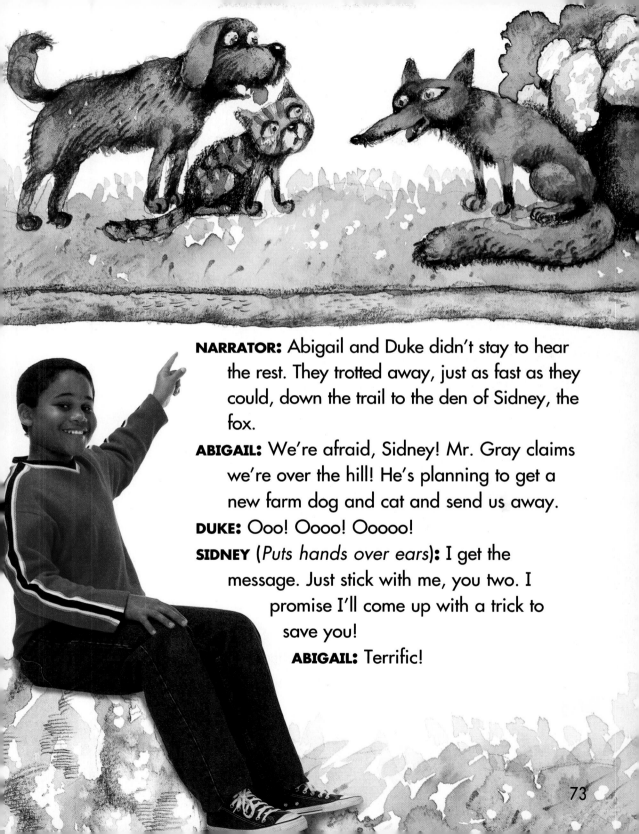

**NARRATOR:** Abigail and Duke didn't stay to hear the rest. They trotted away, just as fast as they could, down the trail to the den of Sidney, the fox.

**ABIGAIL:** We're afraid, Sidney! Mr. Gray claims we're over the hill! He's planning to get a new farm dog and cat and send us away.

**DUKE:** Ooo! Oooo! Ooooo!

**SIDNEY** (*Puts hands over ears*)**:** I get the message. Just stick with me, you two. I promise I'll come up with a trick to save you!

**ABIGAIL:** Terrific!

**NARRATOR:** Do you know much about foxes?
Well, foxes are slick. They don't do anything
for free. Let's see what Sidney has to say.

**SIDNEY:** I have a terrific plan—it can't fail! (*Rubs
his chin.*) It will help you, and it'll get me a
little extra sustenance as well. What do you
say?

**NARRATOR:** See? What did I tell you?

**NARRATOR:** The three animals all went back to the farm. On the way, Sidney got three big rats.

**SIDNEY:** Abigail, jump up on the rail and slip the latch to the hens' shed. I'll put the rats near the grain.

**DUKE** (*Tapping Sidney*)**:** Pant-pant!

**SIDNEY:** Okay, Duke. You can help. Wait until I'm running away, then bark and bay. Make a big fuss!

**NARRATOR:** That fox raided the hens' shed. He got all the eggs for himself!

**DUKE:** Ruff! Rrruff-ruff-ruff!

**MR. GRAY** (*Runs in*)**:** What's up? Well, well! Stamp me and send me airmail! Old Duke kept a fox from taking our hens! Let's keep him!

**MRS. GRAY:** Abigail can stay—she got three rats! Our cat and dog are smart!

**NARRATOR:** Yup! They're smart. But not as smart as that fox!

# Think About It

1. What makes Mr. and Mrs. Gray think that
   Duke and Abigail are smart?

2. Who is the smartest one in the play? Why do
   you think that?

3. Sydney tells a friend about how he helped
   Abigail and Duke. Write what he says.

# A DAY WITH THE ORANGUTANS

by Jeannie W. Berger

You are alone in the rain forest of Borneo, far from any road. The forest is thick, green, and overgrown with vines. Bugs buzz in your ears as you keep looking, looking. Then you hear a tree shake and you stop in your tracks. When you look up, something looks down at you. Is it what you think? Yes, you're in luck! You've found what you were looking for.

It's a baby orangutan! Baby orangutans are endangered. Some are smuggled out of the forest for sale as pets. Some become orphans when people catch and sell their moms. When trees are cut down, all orangutans are in danger. At least this baby orangutan is not one of the rain forest orphans.

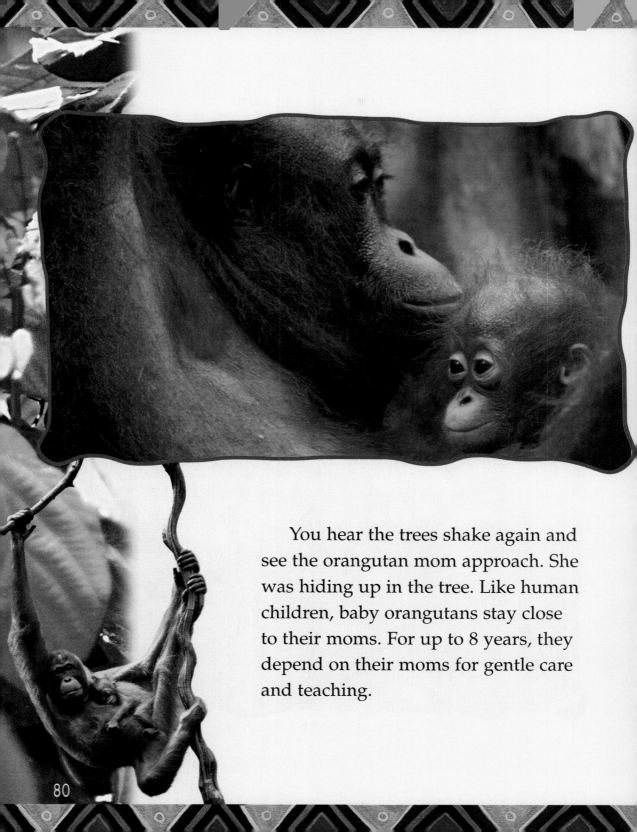

You hear the trees shake again and see the orangutan mom approach. She was hiding up in the tree. Like human children, baby orangutans stay close to their moms. For up to 8 years, they depend on their moms for gentle care and teaching.

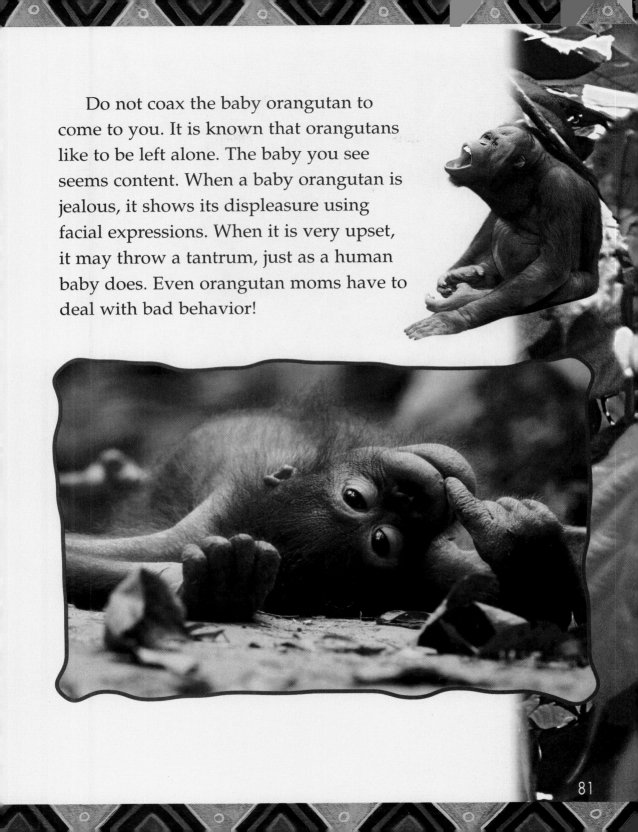

Do not coax the baby orangutan to come to you. It is known that orangutans like to be left alone. The baby you see seems content. When a baby orangutan is jealous, it shows its displeasure using facial expressions. When it is very upset, it may throw a tantrum, just as a human baby does. Even orangutan moms have to deal with bad behavior!

If you can, take a good look at the orangutan's hands and feet. They are just right for gripping tree branches. The baby orangutans must practice swinging from branch to branch. This kind of play helps them develop good coordination. They will depend on this to be safe in the treetops.

The orangutan mom teaches her baby behaviors it will need when it is grown. Each evening, she shows it how to make a nest in a tree. She makes the nest a manageable size for them to sleep in. In time, her baby will practice making a nest of its own. For now, this baby is glad to sleep with its mom.

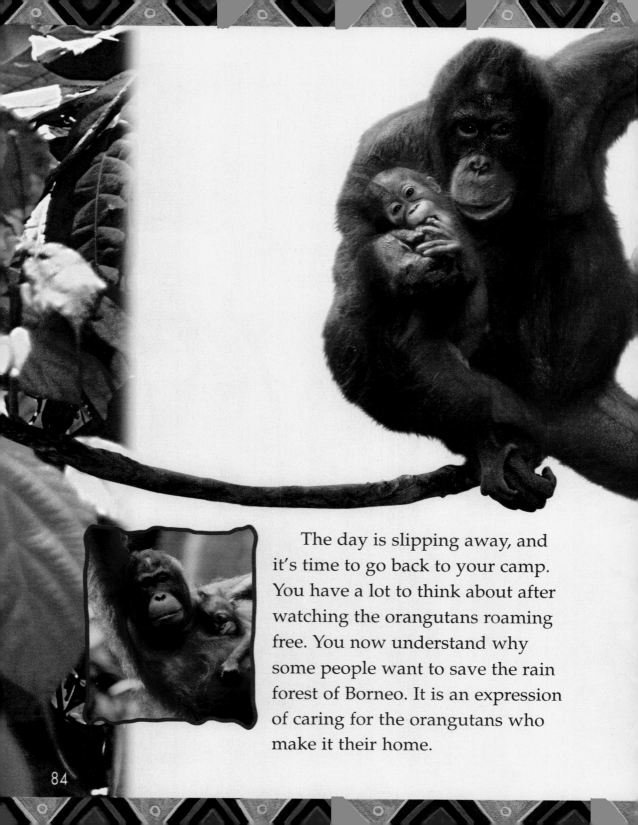

The day is slipping away, and it's time to go back to your camp. You have a lot to think about after watching the orangutans roaming free. You now understand why some people want to save the rain forest of Borneo. It is an expression of caring for the orangutans who make it their home.

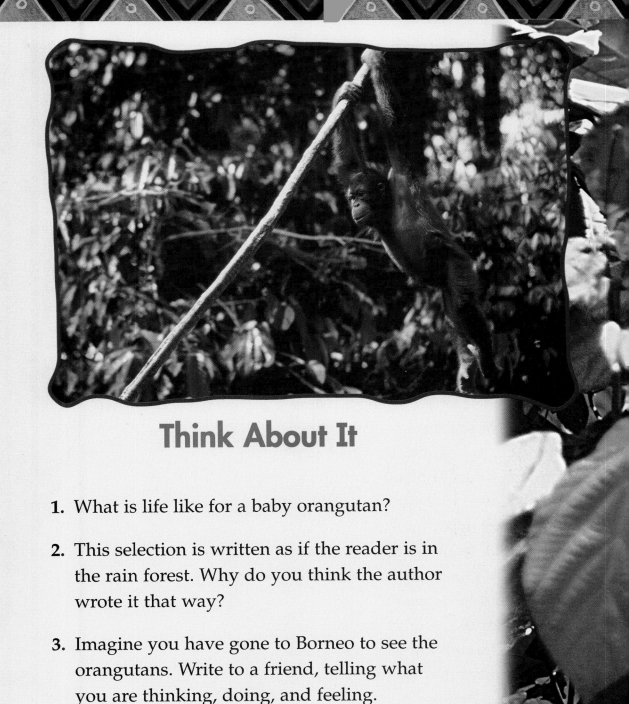

# Think About It

1. What is life like for a baby orangutan?

2. This selection is written as if the reader is in the rain forest. Why do you think the author wrote it that way?

3. Imagine you have gone to Borneo to see the orangutans. Write to a friend, telling what you are thinking, doing, and feeling.

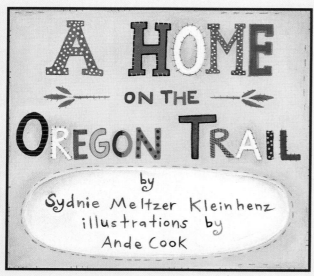

# A HOME ON THE OREGON TRAIL

by
Sydnie Meltzer Kleinhenz
illustrations by
Ande Cook

Kate felt lonely as she brushed crumbles of sod from her pink conch shell. She missed the sea it had come from and her old home in Baltimore. She had loved visiting with neighbors on her front porch there.

The sod dwelling felt almost like home now. The quilts Kate and her mother had hung over the sod added color to the drab walls. Outside, the rippling waves of grass almost substituted for the splashing waves near Baltimore.

Jed ran in. "Kate," he called. "I've got more kindling for our fire. I've got something else, too—a traveling man who needs a meal."

"We welcome all travelers on the Oregon trail," Kate said, smiling. "Come in! No one has visited us in a long time."

"Thank you," the man said. He didn't look very old—maybe 20, Kate guessed. "I'm Patrick Guthrey. I take pictures."

Kate's mother and father came in from the fields. They were very pleased to meet Patrick.

At dinner, Patrick told the family many tales of his travels on the Oregon trail. Then he invited them to pose outside for a portrait. Mother and daughter wore their best bonnets. Kate also wore a big smile for Patrick!

Back inside, they looked at Patrick's prints. His landscapes were splendid.

A rustle distracted them. They looked up as a king snake slid through the sod above one of the quilts! Patrick tossed it outside.

When he came back in, he looked alarmed. "Friends, that glow outside is not sunset. It's a grass fire!"

The two men rushed to beat back the flames. Jed drove the mule and goat to the sod barn. Mother and daughter ran to chase in the hens and gather up the chicks.

Then everyone huddled in the sod home. A wall of fire roared through the windbreak and scorched the paddock. After it had blazed on past the sod dwelling, they stepped outside to look around.

The sea of grass rippled no more. All was smoking blackness. "Thank goodness we're all safe!" Kate's mother exclaimed.

"At least there's time to plant again," said her father. "We'll still get a harvest."

"I'll help you in the fields before I travel on," Patrick said.

Kate's father gave Patrick's hand a shake. "Thank you," he said. "Will you come back in the fall to share our harvest?"

"Of course," said Patrick, smiling at Kate. "I'll have to bring you your portrait."

Kate smiled back at Patrick. She was thinking that she would not be lonely on the plains anymore. It had not been a perfect day, but it had been a perfect visit!

# Think About It

1. Why does Patrick go to Kate's home?

2. Why was the family happy to have a visitor?

3. Write a list of words that tell about Kate at the beginning. Write another list of words that tell about Kate at the end. Then use your lists to write a paragraph about Kate. Tell how and why she changes.

# Draw Conclusions

In "A Home on the Oregon Trail," the author writes that Kate's parents came in from the fields. The author does not tell why they were outside. Sometimes an author does not explain things in a direct way. You have to use what you already know to figure out the author's meaning. This is called **drawing conclusions**.

The chart below shows how you might draw a conclusion about why Kate's parents were in the fields.

| What You Read | What You Already Know |
| --- | --- |
| Kate's mother and father came in from the fields. | Pioneers grew their own crops; crops grow in fields. |

| Conclusion |
| --- |
| Kate's mother and father were working in the fields, taking care of their crops. |

Now read this sentence from the story.

**Kate wore a big smile for Patrick.**

Think about the story words. Think about your own experience. What conclusion can you draw about Kate's feelings?

Write about a time when you felt happy or sad, but don't tell what your feelings were. Give details about what you said and did, and let your readers draw a conclusion about how you felt.

# Sisters Forever

by Ann Chang • illustrated by Tammy Smith

Pearl looked around glumly. She had worked hard to make her bed and bookshelf neat and tidy, but she still felt worried. She had never had to share with anyone before.

"Your new stepsister will be your sister forever," Mom said. "You'll get to like sharing with her when she visits each summer."

"Every summer!" Pearl said to herself irritably. "That'll be a real pleasure."

All the way to the airport to meet LaVerne's plane, Pearl tried to ignore the situation. She was just getting used to having a stepfather, and now she had to get used to having a stepsister, too.

When LaVerne walked off the plane, Pearl gave her a weak smile. LaVerne wore her curly hair long with a bow. Pearl kept her hair short for sports. LaVerne looked like a girl with very different interests from hers. How would the two of them ever get along?

Pearl did not feel more hopeful when her stepsister unpacked her things. First LaVerne put a stuffed toy cat next to Pearl's baseball mitt. Then she cluttered the tidy shelf with her books and the rest of her possessions.

Pearl's disposition changed. She didn't feel happy anymore. She felt that LaVerne was imposing on her. Pearl didn't want to be mean, but she couldn't help feeling a grudge.

LaVerne seemed no happier with the situation than Pearl. At dinner, the girls started to bicker. They both looked angry and sad.

Pearl's stepfather tried to cheer them up. "This summer will be fun," he said. "I like having my two girls together. I wouldn't be surprised if you find you like some of the same pastimes."

The girls just frowned and looked down at their plates. They had to be sisters forever, but they didn't have to like it.

The next morning Pearl got up early while LaVerne was still sleeping. She glared at LaVerne and her possessions, and then she sneaked out. Her parents would want her to take LaVerne to meet her friends. Pearl had no such plans. She ate quickly and left, intending to ignore LaVerne.

Pearl played soccer with her friends all morning. At lunchtime she went home feeling bad. Sneaking out on LaVerne had been mean. Now Mom might make her stay home all afternoon and play with LaVerne and her stuffed toys.

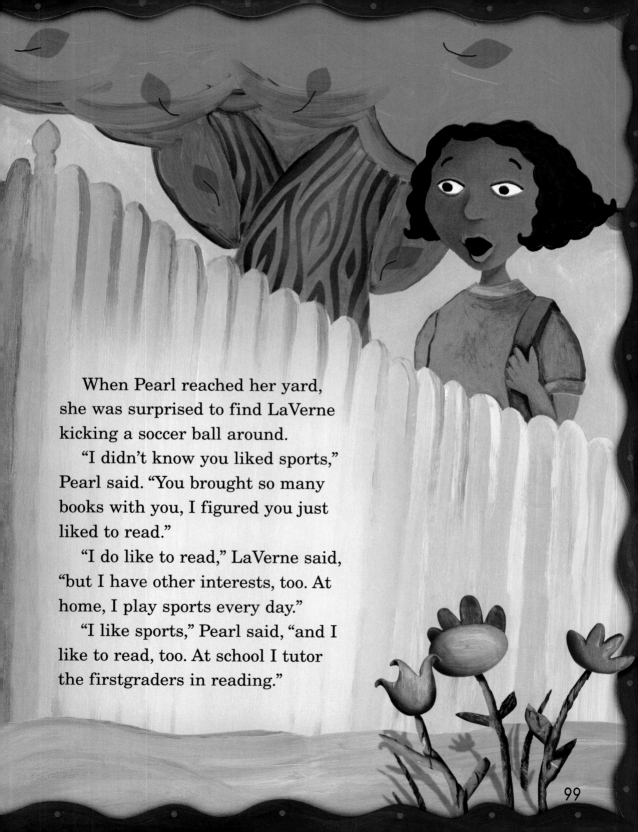

When Pearl reached her yard, she was surprised to find LaVerne kicking a soccer ball around.

"I didn't know you liked sports," Pearl said. "You brought so many books with you, I figured you just liked to read."

"I do like to read," LaVerne said, "but I have other interests, too. At home, I play sports every day."

"I like sports," Pearl said, "and I like to read, too. At school I tutor the firstgraders in reading."

"You can read my books if you want to," said LaVerne. "Do you like to play board games?"

"Yes, I do," said Pearl. "I guess your dad was right. We *do* have some pastimes we both like."

"I guess parents can be right once in a while," LaVerne joked, and they both laughed.

For the first time, the girls gave each other a real smile. The situation was not so bad after all. It began to look as if being sisters forever *could* turn out to be a real pleasure.

# Think About It

1.  Why does Pearl have to share with LaVerne?

2.  Why does Pearl think LaVerne doesn't like sports?

3.  Think about Pearl and LaVerne. Write one paragraph telling how the two girls are the same. Write another paragraph telling how they are different.

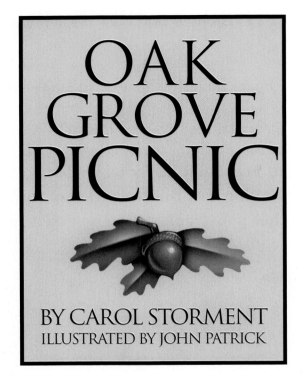

# OAK GROVE PICNIC

BY CAROL STORMENT
ILLUSTRATED BY JOHN PATRICK

The word was out, and before midday the news was all over the field. Everyone had been waiting all summer for this day.

Ruben, a squirrel, heard the news first. He scampered over to see his neighbor, a wood rat named Bo. Bo had been making the acquaintance of several more wood rats. Now, they were all exploring a jumble of dry grass and clover, scrounging for something to eat.

"Guess what!" Ruben called out. "The acorns are ready! It's time to get over to the oak grove."

Bo looked up. "How do you know?" he asked. "It's so hot, I wouldn't want to go all the way over there for nothing."

"I heard the treehoppers talking this morning," said Ruben.

"You mean you were eavesdropping!" Bo said with a laugh. "Why do you believe those insects? What do they know about acorns?"

"They have a talent for finding things to eat," Ruben said. "You know there isn't a bite to be had around here."

"Oh, all right," Bo said. "Let's go before the acorns are all eaten up."

From above, Davis the jay heard the wood rat and the squirrel fussing. Flying quickly, he returned to his nest.

"Hi-ho! It's picnic day in the oak grove!" he shouted to Mavis. "Wake up before our winter's stores are taken from us!"

Mavis looked at him sleepily. "It's too hot to go exploring today," she said, refusing to move.

That sent Davis hopping and flapping around the nest. His antics were familiar to Mavis. Davis was a rather excitable bird.

"Do you want to let those wood rats and squirrels get there first?" Davis's screech was anything but musical, as singing was not one of his talents.

His words, however, were enough to get Mavis up. The two jays set off, keeping a sharp eye out for owls.

The owls could not miss such a racket.
However, they had bigger plans for lunch than
two skinny jays. They knew there would be a full
menu of animals at the picnic! They followed Mavis
and Davis across the familiar fields.

Iris the deer and her baby, Amy, were grazing in a
vacant clearing. Little Amy looked up wistfully at the
musical jumble of birds gliding over, wishing she could fly.

"I wish we had wings, Mommy," she said sadly. "Then
maybe we could find some new green leaves to eat."

Smiling sympathetically, her mother said, "I know you're hungry, Amy. It's the end of summer, so it's logical that everything is dry. When it's picnic day, we'll have . . ."

"I know, I know," Amy said. "The moment the acorns start falling from the oak trees, we can go eat all we want."

Iris told Amy, "The acorns are a treat, but they're more than that. At the end of the dry season, they help us all get fat for winter. Everyone around here will use something from the oaks. Some will save and hide the acorns for the future, and some will eat the leaves. Others will make homes from the twigs. Many of us would not be able to make it through the winter without the oaks."

Amy saw birds, squirrels, and wood rats rushing by. "Mommy, look around! I think it's happening right now!"

Picnic day in the oak grove was indeed in full swing. Bugs were munching leaves. Squirrels and jays were arguing over jumbles of ripe acorns. Everyone ate and ate, while keeping one eye on the owls.

The owls finally had to give up on lunch. They were not used to being awake in the daytime, and they became very sleepy. When the owls went home to nap, everyone else relaxed. Picnic day ended with a lot of buzzing and humming and snoring in the shade under the oak trees.

# Think About It

1. What is picnic day in the oak grove? At
   what time of year does it happen?

2. Why is picnic day so important to the
   animals?

3. Two children sit quietly behind a bush
   and watch the animals at the picnic.
   What do they see? What do they think
   about the picnic? Write your ideas.

# Sequence

Most stories tell about events in time order, or **sequence**. Words that signal time order help you follow the sequence of events in the story. These are some time order words:

**first    next    then    finally    before    after**

Think about how paying attention to sequence can help you understand a story. This chart shows the sequence of some events in "Oak Grove Picnic."

Ruben is the first to hear about the picnic.

Ruben tells Bo about the picnic in the oak grove.

Davis overhears and tells Mavis about the picnic.

Think about the other events in "Oak Grove Picnic." What happens next? What happens after that? What is the last thing that happens?

Choose a story you have read. Think about the sequence of events in that story. Make a chart like the one above to show the most important story events in time order.

# Wolf Pack

## SOUNDS AND SIGNALS

by Kana Riley

A wolf howls across the tundra. Then comes another howl and another across the arctic land. Each wolf makes its own sound. Together, the pack is like a musical group, with each singer sounding a different note.

Wolves live in family groups called packs. Howling is one of the ways the pack members talk to each other.

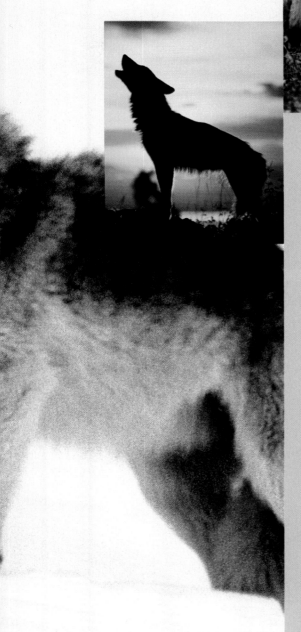

Wolves have a lot to say. Sometimes they howl loudly to call the pack together. At other times the howls say "keep out" to outsiders, wolves that are not part of the family.

Important times call for howls. If a pack member is injured, it howls for help. If the injured wolf dies, all the other wolves howl piteously. When pups are born, pack members howl their pleasure.

In wolf society, howls are not the only way to talk. An angry wolf growls. The other wolves understand this message and know to stay away.

If a wolf is feeling friendly, it may squeak like a mouse. Wolves squeak when they are bonding with each other. A mother wolf squeaks when she talks to her pups.

Like the dogs they are related to, wolves also bark. That sound signals excitement, perhaps at a new scent.

Each wolf pack has two leaders, the alpha male and the alpha female. The alpha animals have ways to signal the others that they are boss.

Sometimes they use their tails. A tail held up shows that the alpha wolf is proud to be the leader. When another wolf meets an alpha wolf, it holds its tail down, showing that it is willing to surrender its power to the leader.

The alphas use other signals as well to show their leadership. An alpha may stare at another wolf or lay a paw over its back until it lies down in surrender. At these times, the alpha's ears will be held forward while the other wolf's are laid back.

To be strong leaders, the alpha wolves must have the cooperation of the pack. Most of the time, using these gentle ways, they can get it without a struggle.

Wolves have abundant ways to display their cooperation. Are pack members licking an alpha wolf's muzzle? Is a wolf holding another's snout in its mouth? Is a wolf wagging its tail? All of these are messages, too. They are ways members of the pack tell one another they are friends.

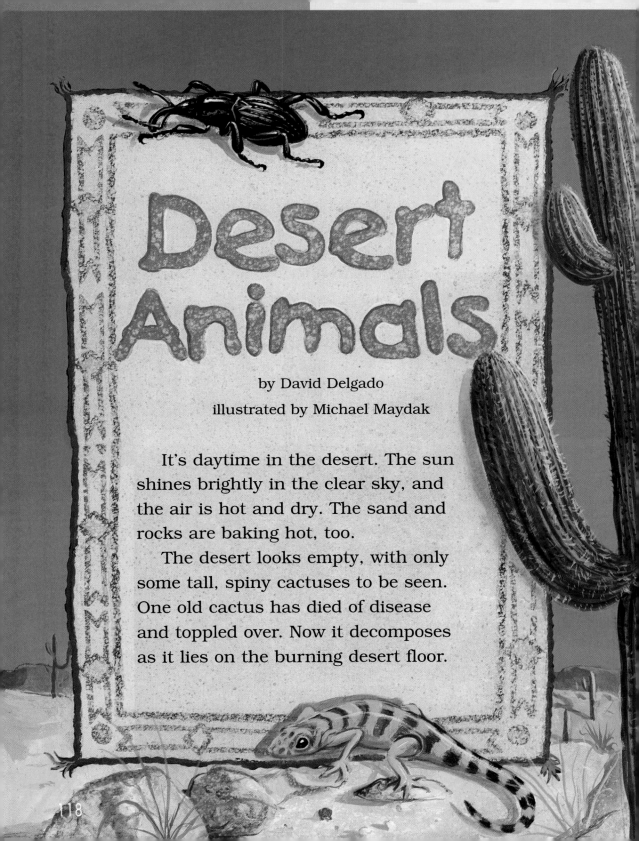

# Desert Animals

by David Delgado

illustrated by Michael Maydak

It's daytime in the desert. The sun shines brightly in the clear sky, and the air is hot and dry. The sand and rocks are baking hot, too.

The desert looks empty, with only some tall, spiny cactuses to be seen. One old cactus has died of disease and toppled over. Now it decomposes as it lies on the burning desert floor.

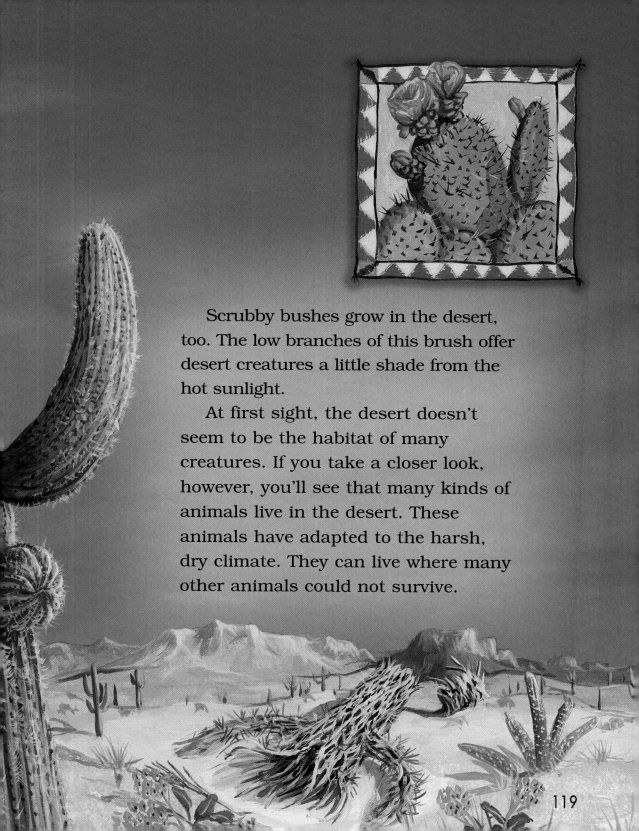

Scrubby bushes grow in the desert, too. The low branches of this brush offer desert creatures a little shade from the hot sunlight.

At first sight, the desert doesn't seem to be the habitat of many creatures. If you take a closer look, however, you'll see that many kinds of animals live in the desert. These animals have adapted to the harsh, dry climate. They can live where many other animals could not survive.

If you stir up the sand, you may find that it is teeming with life. Many insects, such as ants, beetles, and even bees, dig burrows. Staying underground protects the bugs from the blazing sun.

The digger bee makes a long, narrow tunnel beneath the sand. Here it stores pollen for food and lays a single egg. The baby bee will spend many months growing safely underground.

If you look in the shade under the brush, you may see a lizard trying to keep cool. It has climbed up onto a branch to get away from the heat of the ground. The zebra–tailed lizard sometimes runs on its back feet across the open desert. It does this to keep its front feet and body up off the hot sand.

Plodding along nearby is a big, slow-moving reptile that looks like a land-dwelling turtle. The animal's shell protects it from the sun's hot rays. It gets the water it needs from the plants it eats. One of its favorite foods is cactus flowers.

Take another look at the desert. It's far from empty—in fact, it's almost crowded!

You may spy a rattlesnake asleep in the shade of a rock. Rattlers rest during the heat of the day and come out to hunt and eat at night.

The jackrabbit has big ears that help keep it from getting too hot. They provide more skin to let off extra body heat.

You can spot birds in the desert, too. The small birds that seem to hang in the air just above the brush are hummingbirds. A hummingbird in flight is an amazing sight! It hovers in one spot like a tiny helicopter. It even flies backward!

The roadrunner can fly, but it spends most of its time on the ground. As you might expect, it runs very quickly! It eats mostly insects and small animals—even snakes.

The big, dark birds high in the sky are buzzards. They are searching for a meal on the desert floor. These birds don't hunt live animals. They dine on the bodies of those that have already died, perhaps of disease.

When night comes, the desert is almost crowded. Some different creatures are awake now, after the heat of the day.

Insects buzz through the air, and bats fly out to dine on the insects. Coyotes prowl far and wide, hunting snakes, lizards, birds, and smaller mammals. The lonely howl of the coyote is the night song of the desert.

Day and night, the desert is alive with animals.

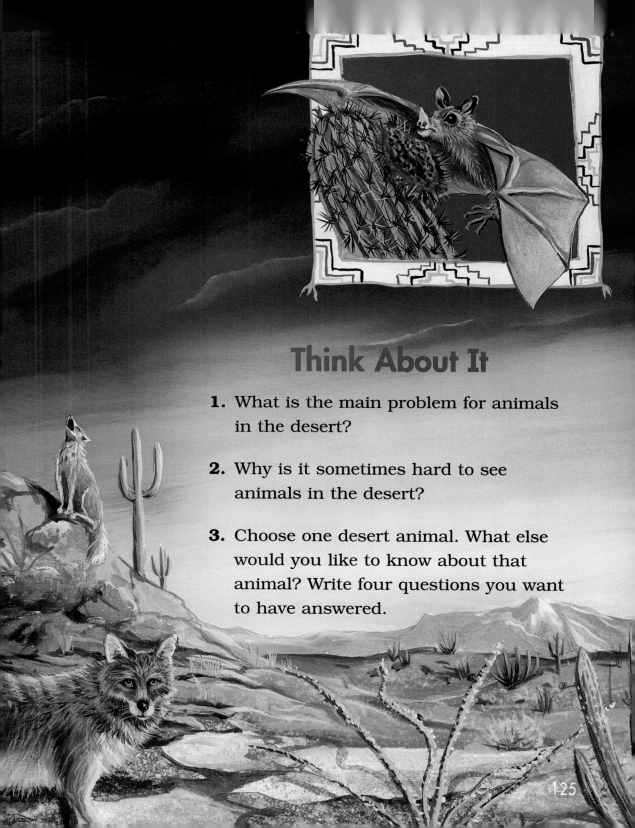

# Think About It

1. What is the main problem for animals in the desert?

2. Why is it sometimes hard to see animals in the desert?

3. Choose one desert animal. What else would you like to know about that animal? Write four questions you want to have answered.

# Who Invented This?

by Beverly A. Dietz • illustrated by Debbie Tilley

Pencils were used long before there were erasers. To correct mistakes, people tried many kinds of things to remove their pencil marks.

Rubber erasers were first used in the 1700s. Still, finding an eraser when you needed one could be a problem.

Then, in 1858, two inventors had the same bright idea. Both Hyman Lipman and Joseph Rechendorfer invented pencils with erasers right on the end of them.

For a long time, shoppers took their own baskets to market to put their food into. Since the baskets didn't have much space, people couldn't get much in one trip.

Sylvan Goldman owned an early supermarket. He wanted shoppers at his store to get a lot of food—more than they could put into their baskets. In 1937, Goldman had an idea. What if shoppers had carts on wheels, carts that could hold lots of food? He invented the shopping cart.

Before 1904, many people ate ice cream—but only out of dishes. At the World's Fair held that summer, the people selling ice cream ran out of dishes.

Ernest Hamwi was selling thin waffles at the fair. He rolled some waffles into cones. People could put their ice cream into the circular opening of the cone. Just like that, he invented ice-cream cones!

John Spilsbury invented picture puzzles more than 200 years ago. He wanted to help teach children about places around the world. He began by painting maps on wood. Then he cut the maps apart so that children could put them together again.

Spilsbury's maps were the very first picture puzzles. Now kids and grown-ups alike put puzzles together just for fun.

Walter Hunt was an inventor. In 1825, he needed some money. A man handed him a piece of wire. He said he would pay Hunt $400 for any invention he could make from it.

Hunt's response was almost automatic. He knew well the problems people had with pins. Hunt invented the safety pin and got his $400. However, the other man then owned Hunt's idea, and it made him rich.

You can see that not all inventions are complicated and expensive. Some of the little things we use every day are important inventions.

Do you have an idea for an invention of your own? You may want to modify something people already use. Maybe you'll invent a brand new device. Then one day someone might use your invention and ask, "Who invented this?"

# Think About It

1.  What have you learned about the reasons people have for inventing things?

2.  How do you think Walter Hunt felt about inventing the safety pin?

3.  You've invented something new, and it's a success! Write a news story about your invention that the local newspaper could print.

# Main Idea and Details

A friend wants to know what "Who Invented This?" is about. When you tell what the story is mostly about, you are telling the **main idea** of the story.

**Details** give information to explain the main idea. Details answer the questions *Who, What, Where, When, Why,* and *How.*

The chart below shows the main idea and some of the details in "Who Invented This?"

| Main Idea | Supporting Details |
|---|---|
| Some of the little things we use every day were invented in interesting ways.  | • The first picture puzzles were maps that were cut apart. They were invented to teach children where countries are.<br>• Ice-cream cones were invented when an ice cream vendor ran out of dishes. |

Think of another supporting detail you could add to the chart.

Plan a paragraph about an invention you think is useful. You may choose one from the selection or another one you like. Make a web to show your plan. In the center of your web, write a sentence that tells the main idea of your paragraph. In the spaces around the center, write words or phrases that give supporting details.

# The Case of the Strange Sculptor

by Lisa Eisenberg • illustrated by Kenneth Spengler

It was an important day in the village of Fudge
Corners. All the citizens had come to the village square to
see the work of a local sculptor revealed. Gina Ginetti,
well-known girl detective, was there with her friends
Angela and Al.

"I'm so excited!" Angela exclaimed. "Today's the day we
get to see Reggie Rodgers's statue of the Gentle Giant. It's
supposed to be his finest work yet!"

"I don't see what all the fuss is about," Al muttered.

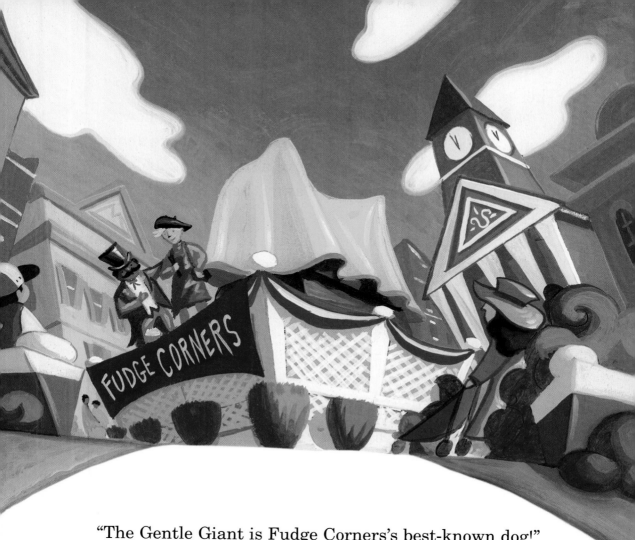

"The Gentle Giant is Fudge Corners's best-known dog!" Angela retorted. "He saved the life of the village's founder, Felix Fudge, in 1809."

"The Gentle Giant is fine," said Al. "It's Reggie Rodgers I don't like. He got first prize in the art show last year, and he's bragged about it ever since!"

Angela frowned. "Maybe the reason you don't like Reggie is that he's a better sculptor than you are!"

"*I'm* the better sculptor," Al insisted. "*He's* just the better boaster."

"Oh, stop arguing, you two," Gina broke in. "Look! They're about to unveil the statue!"

The mayor of Fudge Corners retold the story of how the Gentle Giant had saved Felix Fudge. He also spoke about how lucky their village was to have a fine sculptor like Reggie Rodgers. Then he swept away the sheet that had hidden the statue.

"Ohhhh," cried the crowd. "The dog looks so lifelike! What a genius Rodgers is!" A flock of pigeons fluttered down to investigate.

Everyone clapped, except for Al. His mouth dropped
open and he gaped at the platform. "That's *my* statue of
the Gentle Giant! I made it in my basement, and it was
still there last night. Someone stole it, and I know who's
guilty. Reggie Rodgers, that's who!"

Angela put her arm around her excited friend. "Come on
now, Al. We know you don't like Reggie Rodgers, but that's
no reason to make up wild stories!"

"I *did* make it! I wanted to see if I could do a better job
than Reggie. I was certain I could," declared Al.

Angela glanced nervously around the crowded square. "Everyone is looking at us strangely. You'd better pipe down, Al."

"Wait a second, Angela," Gina put in. "I can't remember Al ever telling a lie. I believe him!"

"What reason could Reggie have for taking Al's statue?" Angela asked. "It doesn't seem logical."

"I don't know, but I trust my detective's instinct," Gina said. "Let's find him and talk to him straightaway!"

Al found the support of Gina and Angela strengthening as they searched the large crowd. When they located Reggie Rodgers, Al marched right up to him. "Why did you steal my statue?" he asked.

Reggie sneered. "Ha! Why would I sneak into your basement and steal your sad little statue?"

"I don't know!" Al yelled. "Maybe yours didn't come out right, or maybe you didn't finish on time."

Reggie glanced around nervously. "That's crazy! I don't even know where you live, and besides, I have an alibi for last night."

"I've done it again!" Gina bragged. "I've cracked another case. Reggie, whatever your alibi is for last night, it's a fake. *You* know you stole Al's statue, and *I* know you're guilty. You gave yourself away twice!"

How did Gina know that Reggie had stolen Al's statue?

**Solution:** Reggie said he didn't know where Al lived, but he knew the statue had been in the basement. Also, he knew the statue had been stolen last night!

# Think About It

1. How is Gina able to solve the mystery?

2. How do you think Reggie feels when the mayor reveals the statue of the Gentle Giant? How do you think he feels when Gina, Al, and Angela come rushing up to him?

3. What do you think happens after Gina shows that Reggie is guilty? Write the next part of the story.

# Just Enough Is Plenty

by Sydnie Meltzer Kleinhenz • illustrated by Normand Cousineau

A farmer earned just enough to live a simple life. Being of a thrifty character, he insisted on saving every extra coin. Over time, his savings grew to a generous sum. He became fascinated with his riches—and highly annoying to his friends and neighbors.

"I'm rich now, but don't worry," he said to a friend. "I'll still talk to you."

Being of a rascally character, his friend saw a chance for fun. "How can I know you're rich," he said, "unless I see some evidence?"

The friend had made a roguish plan with neighbors to stop the farmer from boasting. Now he said, "I seldom boast, but I'm rich, too. I own all the fields on this road."

"Really?" the farmer asked.

"It's the truth," insisted the friend. "Just ask your neighbors."

"Hmm," said the farmer. He set off down the road to investigate. As he passed rows of corn, beans, and melons, he asked his neighbors, "Whose fields are these?"

The neighbors stuck to the plan. They told him the fields belonged to his friend.

The farmer promptly purchased extra land. Meanwhile, the friend borrowed neighbors' pigs and hens. Then he visited the farmer, who was toiling in his new fields. His clothes were soiled and his face was wet.

"Hello," called the friend.

"Hello, friend!" the farmer called back. He pointed to his fields. "Now you see I'm a rich man."

"You will harvest more than enough for a rich man!" his friend said. "I seldom boast, but I'm very rich myself. I've just purchased ten more pigs and twenty more hens."

That night, the farmer crept to his friend's yard to see if he really had more animals. "It's the truth!" he whispered.

The next day, he purchased more pigs and hens. There was a lot of extra oinking and clucking.

The farmer spent the day waving hens away from windows, guarding his crops from pigs, and toiling in the sun.

When his friend arrived, the farmer pointed to the animals and said, "Now you see I'm a rich man." Then off he dashed to guard his corn from hungry pigs. He crept back so tired that he plopped in a chair, smashing an egg a hen had laid there.

"You'll have more than enough ham and eggs for a rich man," his friend said. "Yet this hut of yours does not look like the home of a rich man. No one passing by would guess that you're rich. You need a fine, big house now."

The farmer was annoyed. "What!" he said. "How would I find time to work on a big, new house? I don't have time now even to think." He stomped off.

That night, the farmer did think. He looked around his cozy hut. It was just right for him. He didn't want a big house—or all those fields and animals that made him so tired. He knew what he needed to do.

The next day, the farmer joyfully gave away his fields, pigs, and hens. He was left with just enough, and that was plenty.

# Think About It

1. Why does the thrifty farmer purchase more fields and more animals? Why does he give them away?

2. How do you think the thrifty farmer feels after he gives his fields and animals away?

3. What do you think the farmer's neighbors say when he gives away what he has purchased? Write their conversation.

# Summarize and Paraphrase

If you tell a friend about "Just Enough Is Plenty," you might say:

> A farmer had always been content to have just enough. He saved a lot of money and began bragging about how rich he was. A friend tricked the farmer into buying more fields and more animals. When the friend wanted him to buy a new house, the farmer decided that having just enough was plenty for him.

When you retell just the main events of a story, you are summarizing. A summary of a story is much shorter than the original.

When you retell everything in a sentence or paragraph in your own words, you are paraphrasing. A paraphrase is about as long as the original.

It is helpful to summarize and paraphrase as you read. It helps you think about and understand what you have read.

With a partner, choose four sentences from "Just Enough Is Plenty." Work together to paraphrase, or restate, those sentences in your own words.

# Big Bad Wolf and the Law

### by Deborah Eaton    illustrated by Terry Hoff

**Big Bad Wolf**

## TIME:

*August, some year*

## PLACE:

*Storyland Court*

**Judge Bo Peep**

**Lawyer**

**Bailiff**

**Red Riding Cap**

**BAILIFF:** Order in the court! All rise for Judge Peep.

**JUDGE PEEP:** Be seated. Let's launch right into this. What is the charge?

**LAWYER** *(hands judge a paper)*: Attempted eating, Judge.

**JUDGE** *(discards paper)*: Well, that's original. Usually eating is acceptable, isn't it?

**LAWYER:** Yes, but Mr. Wolf was found chasing a grandma and her little granddaughter.

**JUDGE:** That's awful!

**WOLF** *(worried)*: I didn't do it!

**JUDGE:** Well, let's get on with it. I've been up since dawn *(yawns)*, and I've got lost sheep that have to be caught.

**BAILIFF:** Mr. Big B. Wolf!
Please stand and raise your
right paw.

**WOLF** *(paw up)*: I'm honored to
be here, Your Honor. Allow
me to say that I never saw
such a beautiful judge.

**LAWYER:** I object!
Attempted flattery!

**JUDGE:** I'll allow it. *(looks
in pocket mirror)* It
shows he's truthful.
Now, call your
first witness.

152

**BAILIFF:** Little Red Riding Cap!

**LAWYER:** What caused you to accuse the wolf, Miss Cap?

**RED CAP:** He . . . he . . . *(begins to bawl)*

**LAWYER:** He what?

**RED CAP:** He said my grandma would be *delicious*! *(cries louder)*

**LAWYER** *(triumphantly)***:** You see? He did it!

**WOLF** *(desperately)***:** No! I didn't! I'm innocent!

**JUDGE** *(chin in hand)***:** I'm so worried about my sheep.

**WOLF:** Sheep? Sheep are delicious, too. Usually I like them in mint sauce, but . . .

**JUDGE:** That's it. HE DID IT!

**LAWYER:** And he isn't even repentant!

**BAILIFF:** Haul him off to jail!

**WOLF:** Wait! This is such an injustice! It's the author's fault, not mine! I was just following the original script! My name is really Big *Bill* Wolf! I'm a real sweet pea!

154

**LAWYER:** Ha! Ha! Tell us another one!

**WOLF:** It's the truth! I'm a victim of circumstances. We all are! Just look at you, Judge! You *can't* like that ruffled dress and awkward bonnet. You have them on because they're drawn on you in every story.

**JUDGE:** Well, I . . .

**WOLF:** And you! *(points a claw at Red Riding Cap)* Do you really want to go to your grandma's all the time? Wouldn't you rather go bowling or something?

**RED CAP:** Bowling?

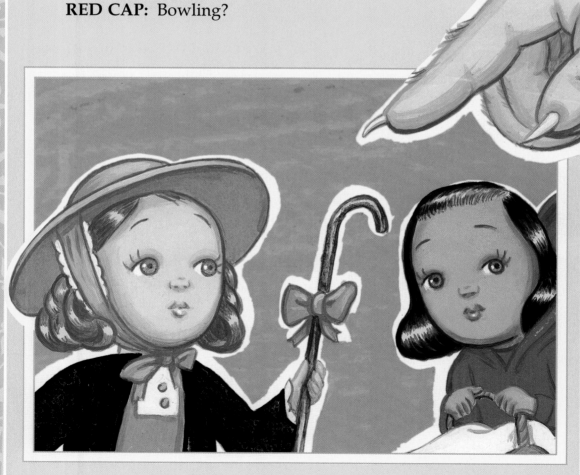

**WOLF:** Aw, I'd never eat the kid, Judge. I'd never put a paw on her.

**JUDGE:** So you didn't eat my sheep?

**WOLF:** Why, I wouldn't hurt a flea. *(scratches)* I'm not big and bad, just ask my mother. Ask anyone!

**LAWYER:** Let's ask my surprise witnesses. *(nods to bailiff)*

**JUDGE:** Who are they?

**BAILIFF:** The three little pigs!

**WOLF** *(sinking into chair)*: Uh-oh.

# Think About It

1. Why is the wolf charged with attempted eating? How does he try to defend himself?

2. Why does the wolf sink into his chair and say "Uh-oh" at the end of the play?

3. What do you think the judge will decide at the end of the case? What will the wolf say and do? Write another scene for the play.

# A Clever Plan

by María Santos

illustrated by
Sylvie Daigneault

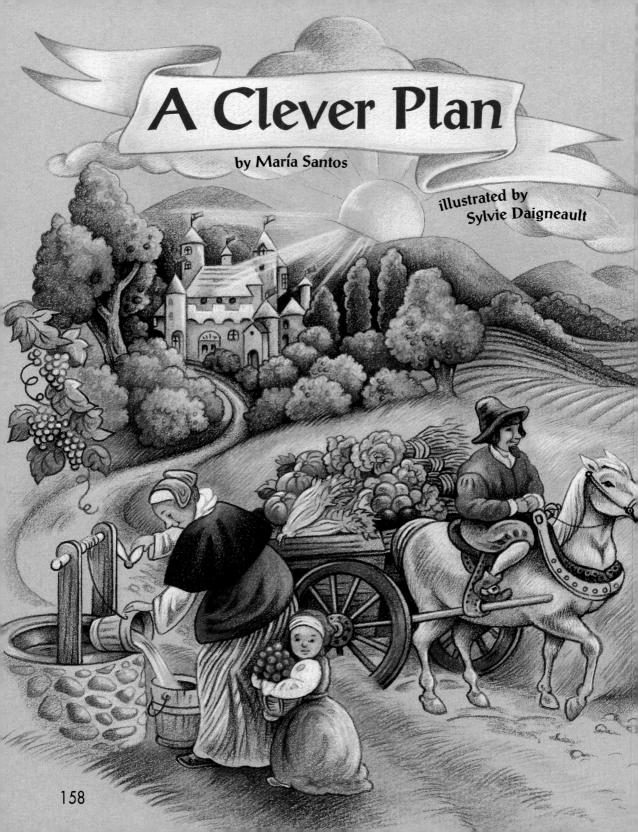

The kingdom of Woodlandia was a good place to live, most of the time. For many years, fine harvests had supplied the people with plenty to eat. Their land was free from famine. Their kingdom was named for its thick woodlands, so, the Woodlandians were also plentifully supplied with firewood. The only problem they had from time to time was their king.

King Roger was kind, as a good leader should be. He believed that kindness was very important. He always rewarded his subjects when they were kind to their fellow Woodlandians.

You might ask, "If the king was so kind, what was the problem?" Well, King Roger had a lot of ideas for rewarding his subjects, but his ideas weren't always clever.

One time a kind shoemaker made a pair of wooden shoes for the king. No shoes had ever fit him as perfectly as these did. "If only my subjects were as lucky as I am," he said, sighing. "They would never again have to put up with uncomfortable shoes." Then a not-so-clever idea came to him.

King Roger proclaimed a royal decree. Everyone in every province of the kingdom was to have shoes exactly like his. For, as King Roger knew, the size and shape were perfect.

The same thing happened when King Roger returned with a pet tiger from a royal journey he took. No pet had ever pleased him as this one did. He decreed that everyone in Woodlandia was to keep a pet tiger. For, as King Roger knew, this kind of pet was perfect.

For a long time the Woodlandians lived with King Roger's decrees because he was such a kind leader. They did not want to hurt his feelings, as he would never hurt theirs.

Things changed when the latest royal decree was proclaimed. This is how it happened. King Roger looked at his newest robe, the one with the satin hood. It was trimmed with a thousand gleaming pearls and a thousand glittering emeralds. It sparkled like a billion stars!

Oh, he looked splendid! Who wouldn't feel happy dressed in outfits like his? To bring this joy to his subjects, he decreed that everyone was to dress as he did.

The Woodlandians stood still. They looked at each other. How could they dress like the king? They did not have silks and satins. They did not have billions of pearls and emeralds.

The mayor of Woodlandia understood the problem. He called together the ministers from every province in the kingdom. They looked through rare old books of wisdom, hoping to find a solution.

After many hours, the oldest minister said, "I have an idea."

"Please, tell us what it is!" they implored. When they heard it, all agreed it was a clever plan.

On the day the new dress code took effect, the Woodlandians went to the palace. They wanted to show King Roger their fine robes. The king just stood there, looking confused. Before long, however, he understood what his subjects had done. He shook with laughter until tears trickled down his cheeks.

King Roger took a walk among the people. He looked at each costume with delight. "These emeralds are . . . ?" he asked.

"Grapes, your majesty," the grocer's wife replied.

"Those plumes . . . ?"

"Twigs, your majesty," said the woodcutter.

"People of Woodlandia," announced the king, "I wish to make a royal decree."

"Oh, no!" whispered the mayor, as he shook in his wooden shoes. "Our clever plan didn't work!"

"I proclaim that from now on, before I make a royal decree, I will meet with the ministers of every province. Perhaps they will tell me when my clever ideas are not so clever!"

King Roger was glad that his loyal subjects had shown him his mistake in this kind way. He rewarded them with a royal picnic in the royal woods, and everyone had a royal time!

# Think About It

1. What problem do the people of
   Woodlandia have with their king?

2. What lesson does the king learn
   about being kind to his subjects?

3. King Roger does not want anyone to miss
   his royal picnic. Create a poster he could use
   to announce the event.

# Fire in the

by Caren B. Stelson    illustrated by Carmelo Blandino

Remember Smokey Bear, the forest ranger's best friend? Smokey always said it was everyone's job to take care of the forest. He said, "Only YOU can prevent forest fires." That's still true, but times have changed.

Forest rangers no longer believe that all fires are bad. In fact, rangers now think that some fires may even be good for a forest.

# Forest

Since leaping flames destroy trees, you might ask, "How can a fire be good for a forest?" It seems that fire is the way a forest renews itself.

Fire burns old branches, underbrush, and diseased trees. The ashes from these make the soil richer, and more sunlight reaches the forest floor. This leads to fast growth of strong, new trees. Today, forest rangers think of fire as an important part of a forest's life cycle.

Deciding which fires to let burn and which to put out is a challenge for forest rangers. If people and homes are in danger, rangers are quick to call in help.

Firefighters and volunteers put on their gear—helmets with face masks and fireproof coats and gloves. They bring their equipment—shovels, axes, and hoes. Planes drop chemicals that make the forest less flammable, slowing the flames. Sometimes the planes also dip huge buckets in a nearby lake and pour water on the fire.

If a fire starts deep in the forest, rangers watch it closely. Often these fires are started by lightning, and most soon burn out on their own. If the wind picks up, however, rangers start to worry. The wind can ventilate the fire and whip up the flames.

Rangers also worry if days have been hot and dry for a long time. With the trees and brush dried out, a fire can get out of control quickly. At times like these, parks may set a curfew so that campers cannot stay overnight. Campfires not put out properly might lead to dangerous blazes.

Firefighters may be asked to stand by for a call. With loyalty and dedication, they stay ready to move in, hoping for rain. Rain is always the best firefighter.

In 1988, rangers faced a serious fire challenge in Yellowstone National Park. It was a hot summer, and the forest was extremely dry. There had been little snow that year, and it had hardly rained at all for six weeks.

When lightning started fires deep in the forest, rangers decided it was safe to let them burn. Then the wind picked up, and everything changed. Flames 200 feet tall leaped and roared. They started new fires and rekindled old ones.

The strong winds sent smoke billowing over the park. Visitors and cabins were now at risk. Firefighters from many cities arrived with their equipment. Brigades of volunteers put on firefighting gear, too. All joined forces, but each time they seemed to have the blaze under control, it rekindled.

The fires raged all summer. Finally, in September, it started to rain, and the fires at last sputtered out. Millions of trees had been lost, but the forest itself had not been destroyed. By the next summer, a new carpet of grass and millions of wildflowers covered the hillsides. The forest had started to heal. The cycle of life had begun once again.

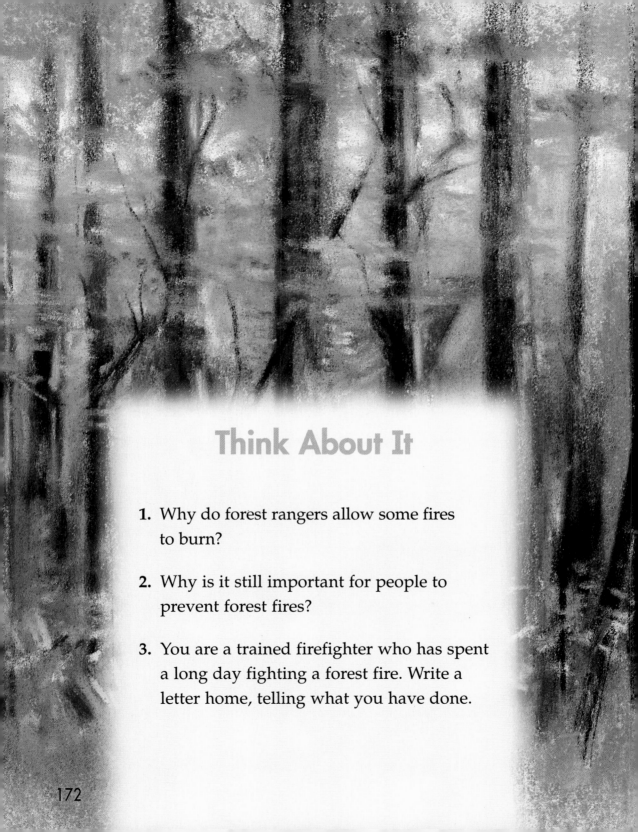

# Think About It

1. Why do forest rangers allow some fires to burn?

2. Why is it still important for people to prevent forest fires?

3. You are a trained firefighter who has spent a long day fighting a forest fire. Write a letter home, telling what you have done.

# Fact and Opinion

**Smokey Bear said "Only YOU can prevent forest fires."**

This statement can be proved to be true. It is a **fact**.

**Smokey is the nicest bear in the world.**

This statement cannot be proved. It tells what someone feels or believes to be true. It is an **opinion**.

It is important to know if an author is stating facts or opinions. Then you can decide what to believe about what you read. If you are reading for information, you would expect to find mostly facts. Newspaper reports, for example, should state only facts.

You might use a chart like the one below to keep track of facts and opinions as you read. To decide whether a statement is fact or opinion, ask yourself "Can this be proved?"

| | Fact | Opinion |
|---|---|---|
| ○ ○ | Fire can be dangerous. | Fighting fires is exciting work. |

Write four sentences about this picture. Make your first two sentences facts. Make your second two sentences opinions.

173

# A Place of New Beginnings

by Ben Farrell    illustrated by Jui Ishida

"This is Ellis Island, Karen," Dad said, "where my father's grandfather began his new life. By coming to the United States, Poppa Joe enriched the lives of our entire family."

"Did he come to this place to qualify for citizenship?" I asked.

"No," Dad said. "He came to Ellis Island as a petitioner to enter the United States. Petitioners were obliged to see an examiner here before going to the mainland."

"Why?" I asked.

"That's one of the things we'll learn about on the tour," Dad said.

We started our tour of the Ellis Island Museum in the Baggage Room. People from all over the world once crowded into this hall. They had to leave their baggage here. I could sense the fear that must have gnawed at them, for their baggage was all they had.

Next, we entered the Registry Room. It was a huge hall, with enormous flags hanging above us. Pointing up at them, I asked, "Is this where the people took the oath of allegiance?"

"No," Dad said. "They didn't take the oath of allegiance until later, at the citizenship hearing. It takes time and study to become a citizen. This was just the starting place."

"I guess I have a lot to learn," I apologized. "What did happen in this room?"

"This is where the examiner checked passengers' documents," Dad said. "Ships had to provide certificates that gave facts about each passenger."

"What did the examiner check for?" I asked.

"They asked where the person had come from and what he or she intended to do in the United States. Doctors had to check the people, too."

"I guess they had to know if the people were healthy," I said.

"Yes," Dad replied, "but they were mainly checking for diseases. They didn't want to endanger the lives of people living in the United States. Immigrants with a disease were sent back to their homelands."

I looked around the hall. How it must have resounded with noise when it was filled with people! Many would be talking excitedly about getting into the United States. Some would be worrying about being sent back.

"Did Grandpop's grandmother come to Ellis Island, too?" I asked.

"I think so," Dad said, "but no one knows what her name was before she married. The tradition of women changing their names when they marry makes them hard to trace."

"That tradition must be changing," I said. "Some of my friends' moms have kept their names. I think I will, too."

Dad laughed and said, "It's a pity they didn't do things that way in those earlier days." I laughed, too, but I felt a little sad about our family history being lost.

Then Dad said, "Just the same, it might be possible to find out about her. We'd have to do some serious digging."

"Let's do it, Dad," I urged. "I'll help—I like doing research!"

The tour guide led us outside to see the Wall of Honor. The names of over 500,000 people who came to the United States are written on it.

Dad asked how he could get Poppa Joe's name added to the wall.

"When we get home," he told me, "I'm going to start the paperwork to qualify him. I'd like to honor him in this way for giving our family its start in the United States."

"After that, can we start researching Grandpop's grandmother?" I asked.

"Of course, we can, Karen," Dad said, smiling. "I'm looking forward to it!"

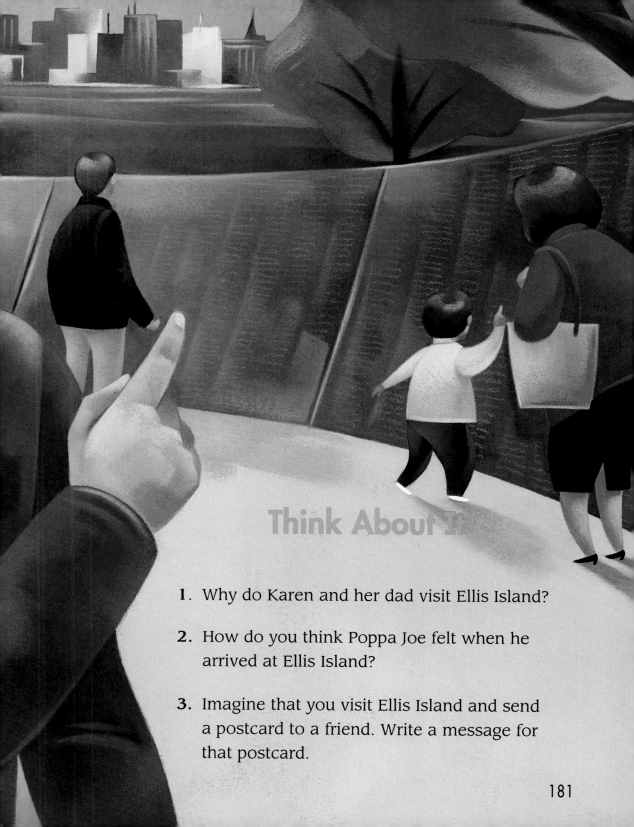

## Think About It

1. Why do Karen and her dad visit Ellis Island?

2. How do you think Poppa Joe felt when he arrived at Ellis Island?

3. Imagine that you visit Ellis Island and send a postcard to a friend. Write a message for that postcard.

181

# One House, Two Families

by Ann W. Phillips • illustrated by Kristin Barr

Once a house stood on a hill. It was a new house then.
Who lived in the house? A mother, a father, and five children
lived there. The children slept in the attic, which was
sweltering hot in the summer. In the harsh winter months the
water froze in the jug by their washbowl. The children kept
warm in their beds under downy piles of quilts. They laughed
and chatted and told stories by the light of a dim lantern.

182

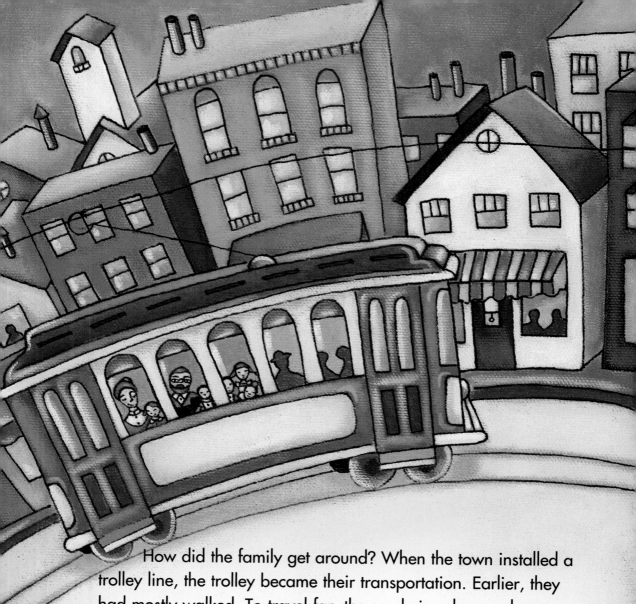

How did the family get around? When the town installed a
trolley line, the trolley became their transportation. Earlier, they
had mostly walked. To travel far, they rode in a horse–drawn
carriage. Most roads were not paved then and were often
muddy or dusty. The trolley made it easy to get to the local
stores.

How did the family communicate? Telephones were new then,
and they did not have one. To send messages long distances, they
had to write letters or, for an urgent matter, send a telegraph.

What did the children do? They helped
with the chores around the house. They
played tag in the yard and hide-and-seek in
the rooms of the house. They wrote funny
verses in each other's autograph books.

One day a photographer from town
took a photograph of the family in front
of the house. They had to stand very still.
They proudly hung the photograph on their
parlor wall. They cherished their house,
which sheltered and protected them.

Years have passed and the house still stands on the hill, but many things about it have changed. Now a mother, a father, and three children live in the house. A telephone has been installed, so the family can make local and long-distance calls. Heating has been installed, too, so the attic is warm in winter. The new children laugh and chat and tell stories at night, just as the earlier children did.

The street is paved now, like all the streets in the town. The family has a car and a minivan for transportation. They can drive long distances in a short time.

The new people are customers at the local stores, but they are also customers at the mall. The new children play tag in the yard and hide-and-seek in the house. They swim at the local gymnasium, too.

The first family to live in the house cherished their home and took care of it. The old photograph of that family was still hanging on the living room wall when the new family moved in. Now a photograph of the second family hangs beside it. "It's a fine old house," the new people say, and they laugh happily because they love it, too. Deep in its floors and rooms and walls, maybe the house laughs with them.

# Think About It

1. Think about the second family to live in the house. Name four things that make their lives different from those of the first family.

2. Why do you think the second family keeps a photograph of the first family in their house?

3. Before the second family buys the house, they see an ad in the newspaper. Write the ad that leads them to purchase this house.

# Author's Purpose and Perspective

Think about why the author wrote "One House, Two Families." The reason the author has for writing is called the **author's purpose**. An author is likely to have one of these three purposes:

| to inform | to persuade | to entertain |

What do you think the author's purpose is in "One House, Two Families"? How would the story be different if the author's purpose were to persuade you that this was the perfect house?

The way the author writes is also affected by his or her viewpoint on the subject. This viewpoint is called the **author's perspective**. It can include his or her attitudes and opinions. Now think about this author's perspective. How does the author seem to feel about old houses?

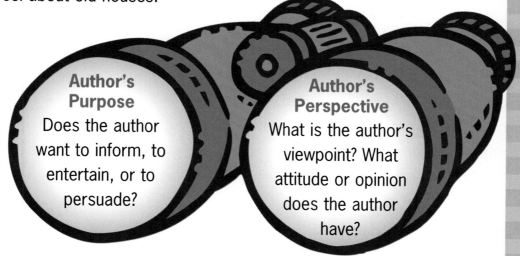

**Author's Purpose**
Does the author want to inform, to entertain, or to persuade?

**Author's Perspective**
What is the author's viewpoint? What attitude or opinion does the author have?

Plan your own paragraph about a house or building you like. Begin by choosing a purpose for your paragraph. Write a sentence that tells your purpose. Then, keeping your purpose in mind, list three or four things your paragraph will tell about.

# School Days

by Susan McCloskey • illustrated by Thomas Buchs

Heather woke with a feeling of dread. Her family had just moved to a new community, and today would be her first day at her new school.

Heather had held her teacher at her old school in high regard and she missed her already. "I just know I'm going to loathe school here," she told herself with certainty.

She raised her head from her pillow and gazed outside. It was dark in the mornings now, and the cars still had their headlights on. The weather was cold, too. Heather snuggled down under the feathery warmth of her comforter.

Soon her mom rapped on her door. "Rise and shine, sleepyhead!" she called out heartily.

"Oh, Mom!" Heather said sulkily. "You don't have to be so cheery!"

Heather got dressed, pulling her red sweater over her head. Her cat was getting ready for the day, too, and she stopped to watch in amusement. He had finished washing himself, but a little tip of pink still protruded from his mouth. That always made Heather chuckle.

"Maybe I should lie and say I have a bad headache," Heather said to herself. "Mom and Dad would probably let me stay home." Then she remembered what her mom always told people. "Completely trustworthy—that's my Heather!" Faking a headache would not be being trustworthy. She was determined to deserve her mom's high regard.

Heather took a deep breath. Undoubtedly she would get through the day, but she was not looking forward to it.

It was her dad's custom to fix Heather a good breakfast on school days. Normally, they both enjoyed this custom. This morning, however, Heather felt indifferent to food.

"A good thing, too," she said, entering the kitchen. "There's no one here!"

She looked out the window and saw her parents laughing with a woman who was walking a dog. The woman looked pleasant and friendly. Heather wished she could join in the laughter, too.

193

Then the woman and her dog moved on, and her parents came back into the house.

"Ready for breakfast?" her dad asked. "What'll it be? French toast? Scrambled eggs? A dry crust of bread?" He was determined to cheer Heather up.

Heather couldn't help responding with amusement. "Just a healthy helping of whipped cream, please. Oh, and a little pie to go with it."

"I can see the headlines now," her dad went on. "Witty Girl Makes Hundreds of Friends in One Day!"

"I wish!" said Heather. "I'd like oatmeal for breakfast, please."

Feeling more cheerful, Heather ate heartily. "Who was that woman you were talking with?" she asked.

"You'll meet her soon enough," Mom said with a smile, picking a loose thread from Heather's skirt.

Just then there was a brisk knock on the door.

Heather opened it. There was the pleasant-looking woman.

"Hi, Heather," she said. "I'm your neighbor, Mrs. Weatherbee. Are you starting school today?"

"Yes, and I'm nervous about it," said Heather. "I'll miss my teacher at my old school. No one could be as nice as she was."

The woman's eyes twinkled as she laughed. "Well, Heather," she said, "I'm your *new* teacher, and I promise to try!"

Heather laughed, too. Maybe school wouldn't be so bad after all.

# Think About It

1. Why does Heather dread the first day of school?

2. Heather sees her parents outside, talking and laughing with a woman who looks pleasant and friendly. What do you think they are talking about?

3. When Heather comes home from her first day at her new school, she writes in her diary. Write Heather's diary entry telling about the day's events and her feelings about them.

# WHEN I WAS EIGHT

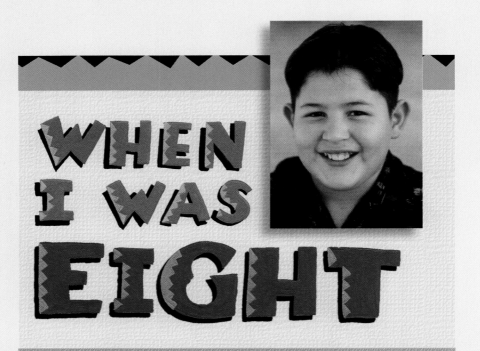

by Roberto Aguas, Jr.
(as told to Diane Hoyt-Goldsmith)

My name is Roberto Aguas (roh•BAIR•toh AH•gwahs), Jr. I have the same first name as my father and my grandfather, so everyone calls me Junior.

My sister and I were born in California and have lived here all our lives. Our parents, however, were born in Mexico. That's why our family speaks Spanish at home and why our Mexican culture is so important to us.

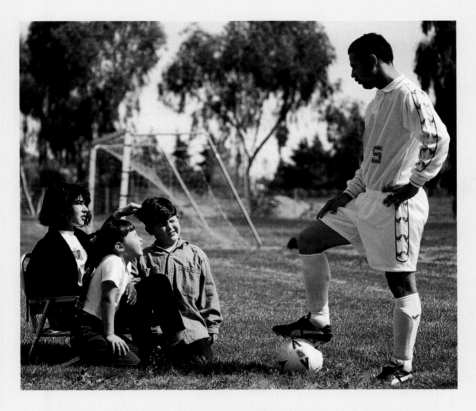

Our grandparents live in Mexico, but we have many other relatives who live in California. Aunts, uncles, and cousins often come to visit us.

When I was eight years old, my grandparents came to stay with us for a month. They traveled from a small town in Jalisco (hah•LEES•koh), Mexico, where they know all their neighbors. I have good memories of that visit because I learned to do something that was interesting and fun!

*Tortillas* (tawr•TEE•yuhz) have always been one of my favorite foods. On that visit, my grandmother taught my sister and me how to make them. For the first time in my life, I helped make the tortillas for a family celebration.

My grandmother used a kind of flour called *masa* (MAH•sah), made from ground corn. She measured it carefully. Then she mixed it with water, salt, baking powder, and lard. She stirred all this into a big, sticky mass.

My grandmother showed my sister and me how to
break off little balls and flatten them with our fingers.
Then they looked like little pancakes!

The rolling out came next. My grandmother put
some masa on the surface of the table to prevent
sticking. When she rolled out a little pancake, it got
bigger as it got flatter. We practiced rolling tortillas
on the floury surface until ours were as flat and
round as hers. We pretended we were cooks in a
Mexican restaurant!

We had a family celebration with the tortillas my sister and I made. We ate them with chile, beans, and a *salsa* (SAHL•sah) made from tomatoes. They tasted delicious! Everyone complimented us on our cooking.

My mother always puts an extra chile pepper on the table for my father. No matter how much chile she puts into a dish she is cooking, he always wants it hotter! My father says that my mother's cooking is better than any you could get in a Mexican restaurant.

While we ate, my parents told us about the celebrations they had when they were children in Mexico. They like to share their memories of the *fiestas* (fee•ES•tahz) in the little towns where they grew up.

Children went to the town square with their cousins and all their relatives. People brought accordions and guitars along, and soon there was music for dancing. The smell of burning mesquite filled the night air as people put steaks on the grill to barbecue.

People ate, danced, and talked to their neighbors. They all had a great time. The next day, the town square was empty. Only the colorful confetti on the ground showed that a celebration had taken place.

Most of the time we still get our tortillas at the store. Just the same, my sister and I are glad that we learned how to make them at home. Now that our grandparents are far away in Mexico again, we have good memories of that happy day.

# Think About It

1. Why does Junior have good memories of his grandparents' visit?

2. How does Junior feel about his Mexican culture? How can you tell?

3. Think about a celebration you have been to, such as a picnic or a party. List the sights, sounds, and smells of the celebration. Write a paragraph to describe what it was like to be there.

# Purple Mountain Majesty

by Deborah Akers • illustrated by Lane Dupont

Many of the first Americans traveled constantly. Hunting for food ruled their lives, whether they lived in the forest, desert, mountains, or plains.

At the foot of a great mountain, there was a place where many tribes stopped to rest. It offered cool springs for drinking and hot springs for soaking. Those who visited left arrows or stones at the pools as they wished for luck in the hunt. They believed that the mountain kept their world in harmony.

Hundreds of years later, in 1806, a man named Zebulon Pike was exploring America's fertile plains and valleys. One day he saw the mountain from far away. It seemed to fill his imagination, and soon he was determined to climb it.

On a summer day, he and his crew set out, believing they could accomplish the climb by nightfall. They found that it took them two tough days just to get partway up! When it started to snow, they turned back. Pike wrote in his journal *No one will ever get up this mountain. It is an awful place!*

Even though he never got to the top, Zebulon Pike was remembered for his discovery. Pike himself had named the mountain Grand Peak, but mapmakers named it Pikes Peak in his honor. In 1820, a man named Stephen Long did make it to the top. When he looked around, he saw a place of endless possibilities.

In 1858, gold was discovered at Pikes Peak. Soon people were reading about this on city corners and in shady country arbors. One thought ran through many heads. *That place could give me everything I've always dreamed about.*

Thousands of people bought mining equipment and made the long, difficult journey across the wild, unsettled land. Soon the mountains were decorated with miners' huts, and makeshift towns sprang up overnight. For a while, the mountain did seem like a place where dreams could come true. People hoisted picks, dynamited hillsides, and searched through streambeds in the hope of finding gold. Life in the mines was very tough. A very few people got rich, but most of the rest lost everything.

When the gold ran out, the miners moved on. Although the mountain was left with holes and gashes, it was still a shining, beautiful place.

In later years, others went to the mountain in search of health. At the time, a disease called tuberculosis, or TB, harmed many people's lungs. Some said the clean, pure mountain air could help heal the lungs of TB sufferers.

Some people got better, and some did not, but all agreed that the mountain was an amazing place. Many people stayed and built a town. Pioneers heading out West often decided to settle near Pikes Peak. For many pioneers, Pikes Peak was their first glimpse of the great Rocky Mountains.

As the town grew, the mountain changed. A cog railroad hoisted visitors to the top, and soon there was a road, too. One thing stayed the same, though. The mountain remained a place of hopes and dreams.

In 1893, a woman named Katharine Lee Bates went to the top of Pikes Peak. She accomplished something wonderful up there. As she looked out at the miles of open sky, her imagination took flight. She wrote in her journal *Oh beautiful for spacious skies . . .* Her words became the song so many would love — "America the Beautiful."

# Think About It

1. Why was Pikes Peak important to so many people?

2. How did Pike feel about the mountain when he first saw it?

3. The beauty of the mountain inspired Katharine Lee Bates to write a song. Think of a beautiful place you have been to or have seen in pictures. Write a poem about that place.

## Vocabulary in Context

As you read, you often come across new words. In many cases, you can read on and use other words nearby to figure out what an unfamiliar word means. Doing this is called using **context clues**. Context includes the sentences and ideas around the unfamiliar word.

The chart below shows how you might use context clues. The possible clues are highlighted in purple for you.

| New Word in Context | Using Context Clues |
|---|---|
| A cog railroad **hoisted** visitors to the top. Soon there was a road, too. | I am reading about a mountain. If a railroad took visitors to the top, *hoisted* must mean "lifted" or "raised." |

Look for the following words in "Purple Mountain Majesty." Use context clues to figure out the meaning of each word. Make a chart like the one above, and write what you think each word means. Then use a dictionary to check your definitions.

arbors—page 208
decorated—page 209
gashes—page 209

# AN AMERICAN LEGEND

by Sharon Fear    illustrated by Gerald McDermott

One day Pecos Bill looked out over Texas and decided it was time to move on.

True, Texas had given him plenty from the time he was a little bitty baby. Hadn't the coyotes of Texas taken him in and raised him when he got bumped off his parents' wagon?

But Bill had repaid Texas. Hadn't he created the cowboy life, holding the first roundup and inventing the lariat and other gadgets?

Hadn't he tamed all the Texas tornadoes by riding them into the ground? Why, a stampeding herd of thirsty giant mosquitoes was about the only trouble left in Texas!

That was the problem. Texas was just too tame for the untamed spirit of Pecos Bill.

"I reckon we'll head west," Bill said to his horse, "and set up a brand new ranch."

Bill went and claimed some land called New Mexico that he figured would do for his new ranch. Then he said to his horse, "I reckon we'll need cowhands."

Bill asked around. "I need men who are rough, tough, untamed, impolite, and disagreeable! In other words, real cowboys!"

"There's a wild bunch fitting all your requirements right up that canyon," said an old-timer.

"Much obliged!" said Bill. He tipped his ten-gallon hat and off he rode.

On the way up the canyon, Bill's horse got spooked. It bucked off Bill and his saddle and headed for home. Right in Bill's path was a rattlesnake of impossible size!

Old softhearted Bill let the snake have the first bite. Then he hollered, "Enough of this nonsense! I'm Pecos Bill, and you're a snake sandwich!"

Bill jumped on the rattler, tied it in knots, and flung it around his neck. "I was needing a new whip to crack," he said, very pleased.

Just then a wildcat of impossible size sprang upon Bill and tried to chew his head off.

Bill was rather annoyed. He jumped up bellowing, "I'm Pecos Bill, and you're a wildcat sandwich!"

This might have meant tragedy for the cat, but with his horse gone, Bill needed something to ride. Before that wildcat knew what was happening, Bill threw his saddle on it and jumped aboard. He rode that cat, bucking and screeching, till it was meek as a kitten.

"Thanks," said Bill. "I enjoyed that."

Bill rode on until he saw some men boiling up beans and coffee over a campfire. They were as big as grizzlies and twice as mean-looking. That may have been because they were surrounded by swirling clouds of mosquitoes. Bill cracked his rattlesnake whip, and the pesky critters hightailed it out of there.

"Howdy, boys," said Bill. "I'm mighty hungry and thirsty. How about a ration of that grub?"

He reached into the boiling beans, grabbed some, and gobbled them. He tipped up the coffeepot and swigged down the boiling brew.

"Now, boys," he said, wiping his chin with a prickly pear cactus, "who's boss around here?"

They looked at the man who rode a wildcat, cracked a rattlesnake whip, swallowed boiling grub, and used a cactus for a napkin. Those cowpokes knew that this was a fateful moment for them.

"You are!" they said.

From then on those boys were as loyal as puppies to Bill. They helped him set up one ranch and then moved on with him to another. Just as the legends about Pecos Bill endure, so, too, that ranch endures to this day.

It's called Arizona.

# Think About It

1. Why do the wild bunch of men agree to work for Pecos Bill?

2. How do you think the rattlesnake feels when it first sees Pecos Bill? How do you think it feels when he says, "I was needing a new whip to crack"?

3. Choose one of the things Pecos Bill does before he leaves Texas. Write your own story about how Pecos Bill does that.

# The Same but Different

by Pam Zollman    illustrated by Winson Trang

"I'm going to Vietnam!" I told my friend Yen excitedly. "You have to tell me about your country. It's so different from the United States."

Yen smiled, mischief in her eyes. "When you picture Vietnam, do you think of tiny villages of bamboo huts? Do you see canoes loaded with fruits and vegetables, traveling down the river to town?"

I nodded. "I think of rice fields, too, with women in cone-shaped straw hats, pulling weeds."

Pacific
Ocean

Rice is a major crop in Vietnam. These women are wearing traditional bamboo hats.

"Farm life is still like that in Vietnam, but my country is growing and changing. Our cities are becoming more like your cities," Yen explained.

"Are you saying we're not really so different?" I asked.

Yen nodded. "The rice fields in Texas south of Houston are the equivalent of Vietnamese rice fields. Americans use fancy irrigation equipment to get water to the fields, but it's the same difference."

"*Same difference*," I repeated with a chuckle. "That always makes me laugh! It sounds impossible."

"It's true about the rice fields, though," Yen said.

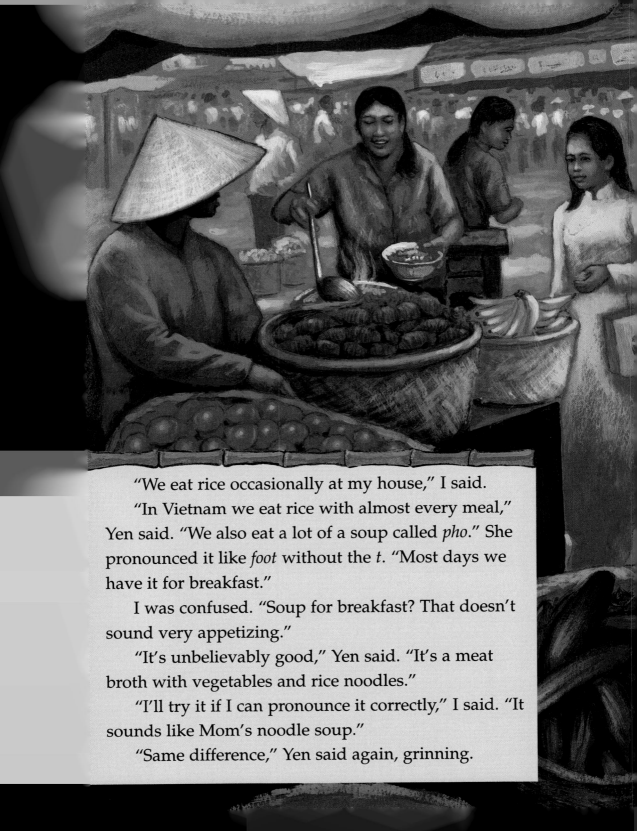

"We eat rice occasionally at my house," I said.

"In Vietnam we eat rice with almost every meal," Yen said. "We also eat a lot of a soup called *pho*." She pronounced it like *foot* without the *t*. "Most days we have it for breakfast."

I was confused. "Soup for breakfast? That doesn't sound very appetizing."

"It's unbelievably good," Yen said. "It's a meat broth with vegetables and rice noodles."

"I'll try it if I can pronounce it correctly," I said. "It sounds like Mom's noodle soup."

"Same difference," Yen said again, grinning.

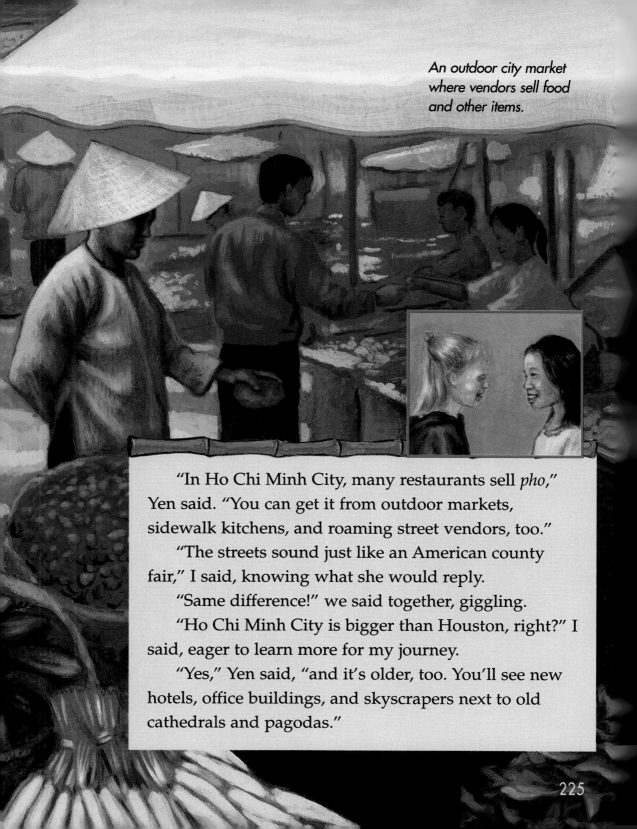

An outdoor city market where vendors sell food and other items.

"In Ho Chi Minh City, many restaurants sell *pho*," Yen said. "You can get it from outdoor markets, sidewalk kitchens, and roaming street vendors, too."

"The streets sound just like an American county fair," I said, knowing what she would reply.

"Same difference!" we said together, giggling.

"Ho Chi Minh City is bigger than Houston, right?" I said, eager to learn more for my journey.

"Yes," Yen said, "and it's older, too. You'll see new hotels, office buildings, and skyscrapers next to old cathedrals and pagodas."

225

"Do you have traffic problems, too?" I asked. "Are the streets crowded with cars and trucks, as they are here?"

Yen nodded. "With everything but canoes! Most people ride bicycles and scooters, though, so add thousands of those with their loud bells. The streets are really noisy. You wouldn't believe the commotion!"

"Can it be any worse than Houston's rush-hour commotion?" I asked with a hint of mischief.

Yen laughed. "You're right—same difference!"

Rush hour in Ho Chi Minh City. Bicycles and scooters are the most popular forms of transportation. The bicycle at the right is a kind of taxi called a cyclo.

"I'm eager to start packing," I said, "but I'm confused about what to take."

"In the city, you'll see many people in jeans and shirts, just like Americans," Yen said. "Shorts aren't considered tasteful for women and girls though, so take some cool sundresses."

"I'm feeling a little overwhelmed," I confessed. "I wish you could travel with me as my interpreter."

"I could help you pronounce words correctly so that people wouldn't laugh hysterically," Yen teased.

I grinned. I knew the people I'd meet in Vietnam would be friendly. The culture might be new to me, but the kids? Same difference!

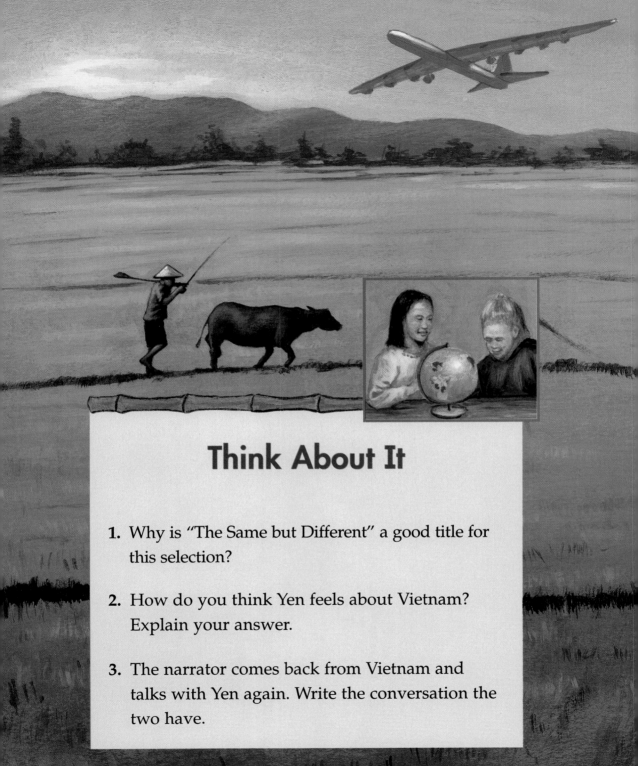

# Think About It

1. Why is "The Same but Different" a good title for this selection?

2. How do you think Yen feels about Vietnam? Explain your answer.

3. The narrator comes back from Vietnam and talks with Yen again. Write the conversation the two have.

# Graphic Sources

"The Same but Different" contains pictures that show what life is like in Vietnam. Captions tell more about each picture.

Sometimes it is helpful to show information in ways other than words. These sources of information are called **graphic sources**, or just **graphics**. Graphic sources include such things as graphs, charts, diagrams, and time lines.

Look at the two graphics below. Think about the kinds of information each one gives.

**A.**

handlebar — seat — reflector — wheel spokes — wheel with rubber tire — gear chain — pedal

**B.**

| How Grade 4 Gets to School | | | |
|---|---|---|---|
| Bus | Car Pool | Bicycle | Walking |
| 10 | 3 | 6 | 7 |

Choose either the diagram or the chart above. Write a paragraph that tells about the information given in the graphic. Do you think the paragraph works well by itself? How does the graphic help?

# BUG CATCHERS

by Robert Newell

illustrated by Doug Bowles

## BROWN BAT

Brown Bat is my name, and bug-catching is my game! Come along and watch me in action.

Marshes are my favorite places to hunt. The boggiest marshes, where water oozes up through the mud, are the best because they have the most mosquitoes. I'm headed in the direction of a boggy marsh right now. It's a dark, moonless night, but that won't slow me down.

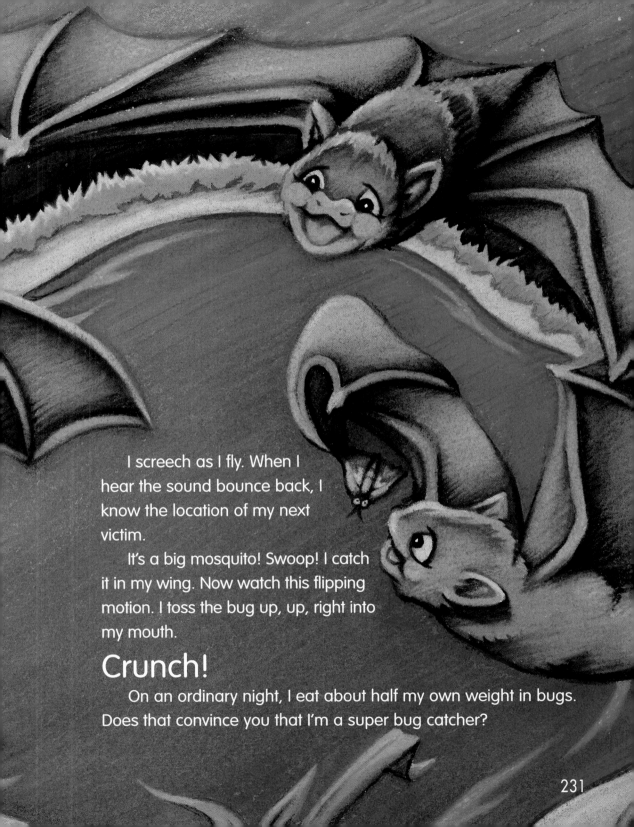

I screech as I fly. When I hear the sound bounce back, I know the location of my next victim.

It's a big mosquito! Swoop! I catch it in my wing. Now watch this flipping motion. I toss the bug up, up, right into my mouth.

## Crunch!

On an ordinary night, I eat about half my own weight in bugs. Does that convince you that I'm a super bug catcher?

# BOLAS SPIDER

Spiders are bug catchers, too. Ordinary spiders use webs, but not me. I use a different invention.

First I perch on a branch by the garden shed, where fertilizers and bug chemicals are stored. Then I let a silky string ooze from my spinnerets. I add a sticky blob to one end to make a bolas, like the ones South American cowboys use. Then I get into position.

What I do next takes great skill and concentration. I don't see well, but I can feel when moths fly by. They have no notion that I'm here. When one comes close, I quickly toss my bolas in its direction.

# I got one!

The moth is tangled in the bolas string. When I pull it in, it's dinner time!

Sometimes I wrap my catch in silk and hang it up to eat later. These roll-ups make great convenience foods for days when I accidentally miss with my bolas. I simply inject a little of my bug-dissolving solution into a prepackaged meal. Then I sip up a delicious dinner.

# PRAYING MANTIS

Why fly back and forth all night or struggle with a tangled, sticky string? I catch bugs by holding still and letting them come to me.

First I have to make a decision about where to wait. Today I station myself on a twig near the ground.

I sit motionless, still as a stone. I have five eyes, and my good vision helps me watch for victims.

# Here comes a beetle!

I wait, and I wait some more. When the beetle is very close, I pounce. Each of my front legs snaps shut at the joint like a steel trap. The beetle's reaction is to kick and wiggle, but it's useless for it to struggle. I will never let go of my dinner.

I will eat the beetle, but I will still be hungry. I am always hungry. Luckily, there are always more bugs.

# OTHER BUG CATCHERS

I catch bugs, too, but I have no intention of eating any. No chocolate-covered ants for me, thank you! I just look at the bugs and let them go.

Anteaters slurp up ants. Fish and frogs gulp down flies. Foxes avoid starvation by eating grubs when they must. All these carnivorous creatures help keep the insect population down, and I'm convinced that's a good thing. After all, how many mosquitoes and flies do you want in your backyard?

## Thank you, bug catchers!

# Think About It

1. How do a brown bat, a bolas spider, and a praying mantis catch bugs?

2. How does the girl who catches bugs feel about the animal bug catchers? How can you tell?

3. Imagine that you're a mosquito. Write about how you feel when you see a brown bat heading toward you. What do you do? What finally happens?

# Air Force Kids

by Sal Ortega    illustrated by Tom Foty

Dear Paul,

Our teacher interrupted classes today to share your letter with us. She liked your idea of writing to investigate what your new environment will be like. I volunteered to write back to you. Air Force kids need to stick together!

In three months, we'll welcome you to our class. Until then, you can ask me about Spain and our base. It's a nice place— you'll like it here.

What's it like in Alaska? Not one kid in Grade 4 has been stationed in Alaska. We're all curious about it.

Your future classmate,

Ricardo Ramos

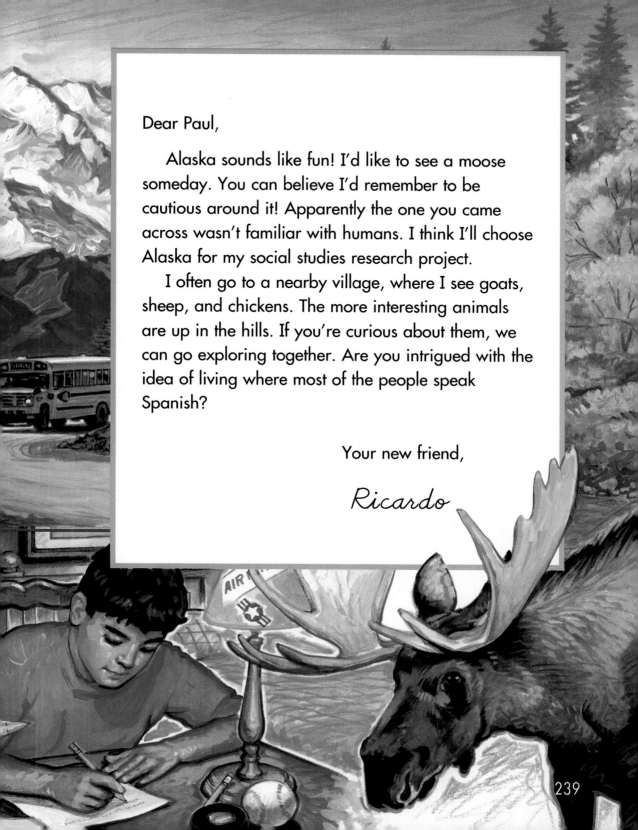

Dear Paul,

Alaska sounds like fun! I'd like to see a moose someday. You can believe I'd remember to be cautious around it! Apparently the one you came across wasn't familiar with humans. I think I'll choose Alaska for my social studies research project.

I often go to a nearby village, where I see goats, sheep, and chickens. The more interesting animals are up in the hills. If you're curious about them, we can go exploring together. Are you intrigued with the idea of living where most of the people speak Spanish?

Your new friend,

Ricardo

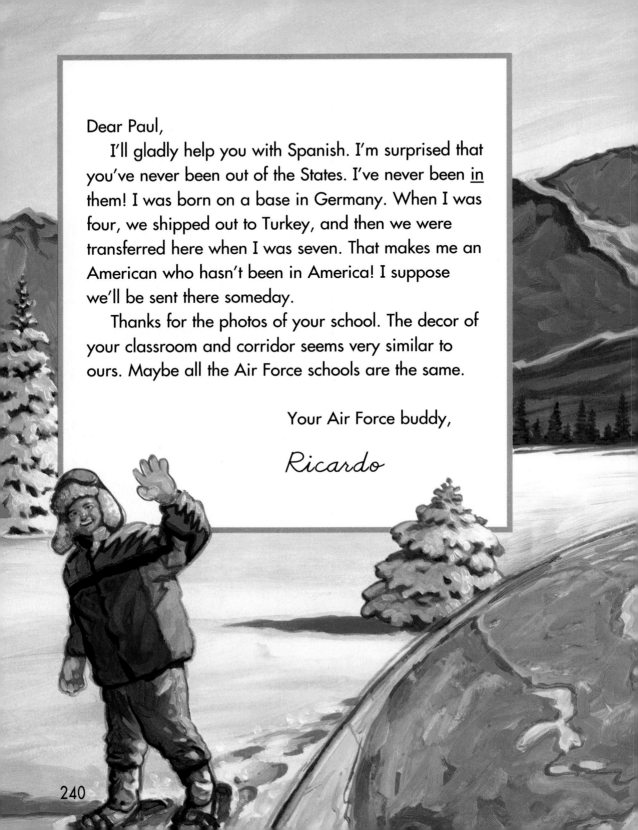

Dear Paul,

I'll gladly help you with Spanish. I'm surprised that you've never been out of the States. I've never been <u>in</u> them! I was born on a base in Germany. When I was four, we shipped out to Turkey, and then we were transferred here when I was seven. That makes me an American who hasn't been in America! I suppose we'll be sent there someday.

Thanks for the photos of your school. The decor of your classroom and corridor seems very similar to ours. Maybe all the Air Force schools are the same.

Your Air Force buddy,

*Ricardo*

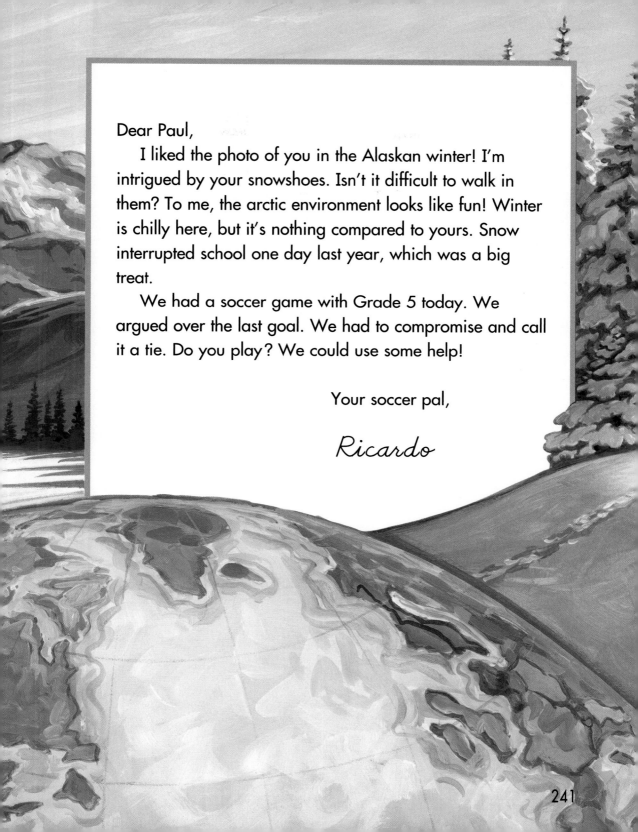

Dear Paul,

    I liked the photo of you in the Alaskan winter! I'm intrigued by your snowshoes. Isn't it difficult to walk in them? To me, the arctic environment looks like fun! Winter is chilly here, but it's nothing compared to yours. Snow interrupted school one day last year, which was a big treat.

    We had a soccer game with Grade 5 today. We argued over the last goal. We had to compromise and call it a tie. Do you play? We could use some help!

                Your soccer pal,

*Ricardo*

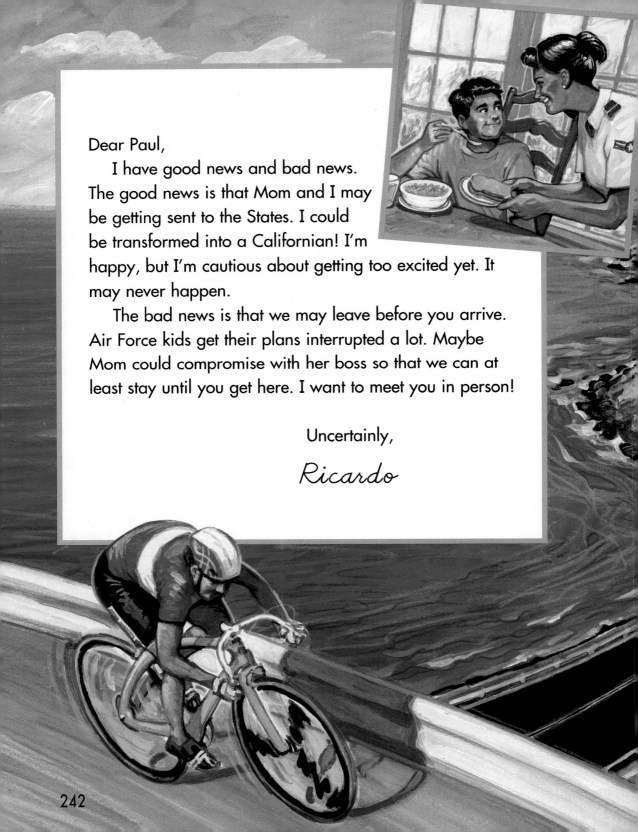

Dear Paul,

I have good news and bad news. The good news is that Mom and I may be getting sent to the States. I could be transformed into a Californian! I'm happy, but I'm cautious about getting too excited yet. It may never happen.

The bad news is that we may leave before you arrive. Air Force kids get their plans interrupted a lot. Maybe Mom could compromise with her boss so that we can at least stay until you get here. I want to meet you in person!

Uncertainly,

Ricardo

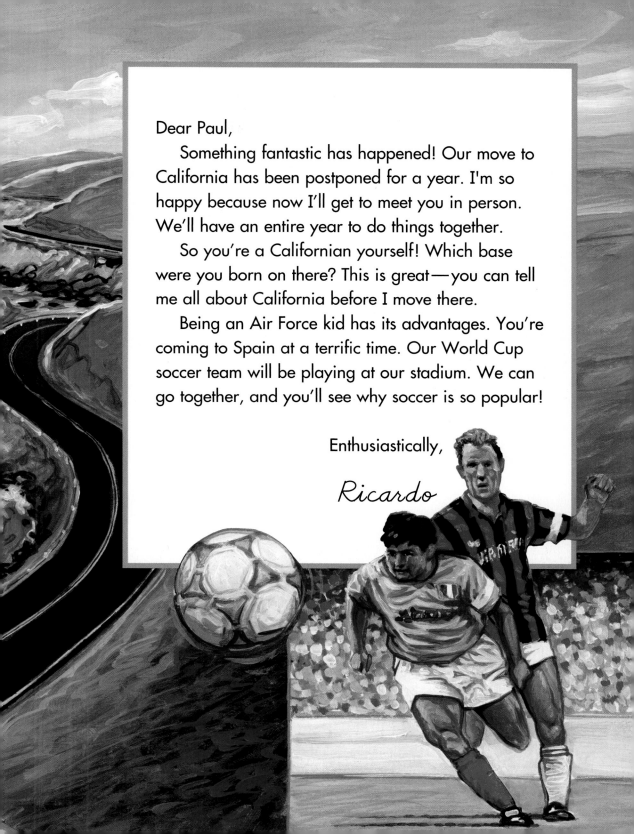

Dear Paul,

   Something fantastic has happened! Our move to California has been postponed for a year. I'm so happy because now I'll get to meet you in person. We'll have an entire year to do things together.

   So you're a Californian yourself! Which base were you born on there? This is great—you can tell me all about California before I move there.

   Being an Air Force kid has its advantages. You're coming to Spain at a terrific time. Our World Cup soccer team will be playing at our stadium. We can go together, and you'll see why soccer is so popular!

                                    Enthusiastically,

                                    *Ricardo*

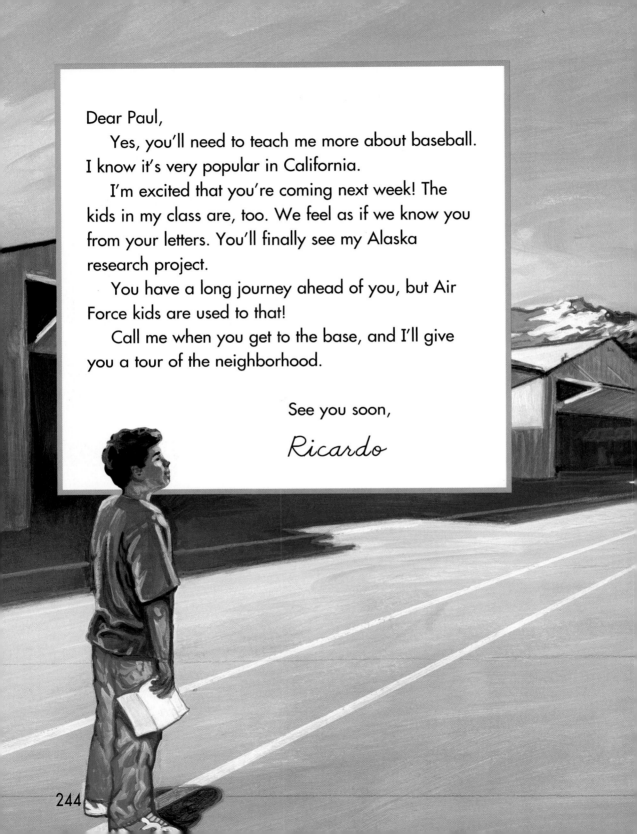

Dear Paul,

Yes, you'll need to teach me more about baseball. I know it's very popular in California.

I'm excited that you're coming next week! The kids in my class are, too. We feel as if we know you from your letters. You'll finally see my Alaska research project.

You have a long journey ahead of you, but Air Force kids are used to that!

Call me when you get to the base, and I'll give you a tour of the neighborhood.

See you soon,

*Ricardo*

# Think About It

1. Why does Ricardo want to stay in Spain until Paul arrives?

2. How do you think Paul will feel on his first day of school in Spain? Why?

3. After Ricardo moves to California, Paul writes him a letter from Spain. Write the letter Paul sends.